Awkward:

Confessions from the workplace

Tom Harrison

Copyright © 2023 Tom Harrison

All rights reserved.

The names of people, organisations and locations involved have been changed to maintain anonymity.

ISBN: 9798856569192

Cover art © Marina Skutina

All rights reserved. Used with permission.

All you need in this life is ignorance and confidence, and then success is sure.

Mark Twain

Contents

Preface	1
Faux pas 1 The perils of fatigue	5
Faux pas 2 The hand dryer	11
Faux pas 3 Synchronicity	19
Faux pas 4 Know your brands	23
Faux pas 5 Caption time	27
Faux pas 6 Interview propositioning	35
Faux pas 7 Putting the D in BBC	43
Faux pas 8 It's all in the name	57
Faux pas 9 Discrete entrances	65
Faux pas 10 The writing's on the ~~wall~~ turd	77
Faux pas 11 The lost art of miming	85
Faux pas 12 Mum's the word	91
Faux pas 13 Shortcuts in IT = shortcuts to P45	97
Faux pas 14 Spell check is not a safety net	105

Faux pas 15 C U Next Tuesday? No you won't, you're fired	117
Faux pas 16 The magnets	127
Faux pas 17 The blood blister	141
Faux pas 18 The headphones debacle	157
Faux pas 19 Deep-bedding gone wrong	167
Faux pas 20 When the evidence is in plain sight	173
Faux pas 21 The Westminster screenshot	181
Faux pas 22 Eat, drink, work, repeat	201
Faux pas 23 Polos - the ~~mint~~ hedge with the hole	215
Faux pas 24 Never get caught	231
Faux pas 25 Conference conflict	237
Faux pas 26 The perils of X-ray vision	253
Dishonourable mentions	261
Self-reflection	269

Preface

There are people who thrive in the jobs they hold, holding their heads high above the surface of the corporate ocean. They tread the water of respectable behaviour with ease.

Then there are those people who struggle to keep even their eyes above the surface, wildly thrashing around like a cat who's been dropped into said water. Where the ability to toe the corporate line, behave like a responsible adult and emerge from interactions with colleagues without an air of awkwardness hanging over them is not so much a foreign concept but an interstellar one.

I am very much one of the latter.

Across a relatively short period in my career I have managed to amass a wealth of awkward, surprising, laughable and downright embarrassing experiences in the workplace. I still cringe about these faux pas to this day and whilst thankfully I no longer work with most of the people involved in these incidents, my friends and colleagues have recommended that I share them as part of a cathartic process to help remove some of the shame I feel whenever we conjure up these memories. A kind of therapy for my professional soul, if you will.

And so across the following chapters I will share with you these little gems from my past. May you find them as funny as my friends did, and not as awkward as my HR managers did… I think if you're the kind of person who enjoys watching people fall down/off/over something (that's YouTube for everyone under 30 and You've Been Framed for everyone over 30) then you'll enjoy it - it is *schadenfreude* at its purest. Go ahead, look it up, it's the best German word you'll ever learn, I promise.

Which brings me to, well, me - there's a few things I'll recount which whilst entertaining for you don't exactly make for pleasant reading for my former, current, and (depending on how badly things go) possibly future employers and colleagues. These are not my finest hours, and so I'd quite like to continue to be able to work with my coworkers without fear of being shunned or worse - I'm fairly certain if my real name was plastered all over this I'd be ostracised, ridiculed or both, much like my young colleague we shall simply refer to as Colleague M who was discovered to have been going at it with a very mature canteen lady like a rat up a drain pipe. Shame on you M, shame on you indeed.

So, in a bid to avoid such shame I'm sharing all of this under a pseudonym. It's a tricky one, picking your pseudonym. Kind of like naming your children, just a tad more stressful. Do I go for a play on words? Or do I pick something that sounds like a barrister and oozes class? Or do I use that old chestnut of the homemade pornstar name? You know, the one where you take your first pet's name along with the name of the street you grew up on, combine them together and boom - you've got your stage name! No, not for me. Instead I decided to take inspiration from two of the all-time movie greats and heroes of the 80s - Cruise and Ford. And then, deciding the name Cruise Ford was utterly shit, I decided to go with Tom Harrison instead - bingo.

And with that I hope you enjoy the sneak peek into my career and the disastrously wonderful world of my faux pas.

Faux pas 1

The perils of fatigue

Mornings are not my friend.

Being woken from my beautiful, dreamy slumber by my alarm is a crushing moment that hits with the same intensity each and every morning. After that, keeping my eyes open, my brain awake and my body functioning is no mean feat - it takes a shower so cold and intense it could be listed in the CIA's enhanced-interrogation catalogue, a coffee so pure it surely contains one of Columbia's other notable exports, and the willpower of a saint.

Starting work before 9am did not bode well.

At the time I worked in a lab developing products that required the use of some pretty scary chemicals (it's amazing how many of the ingredients used to make certain types of plastics can render you sterile or cause cancer…) and some even scarier machinery, so all of my willpower was spent on staying focussed enough to make sure I didn't maim myself or one of my far more alert colleagues. When it came to my breaks, however, my brain could drift off once again into the momentary bliss of a micro sleep. Apparently this is a real thing – where you are seemingly present, but not present, namely because your brain has shuffled off back to bed but left your body in cruise control. In my office-based roles, this represents about 80% of my working state. I'm the consummate professional, I'm sure you'll agree.

On this fateful day I was about to start my lunch break. Having spent the past two hours carefully controlling a chemical reaction that had the potential to easily spiral out of control and make our company look like a clumsy outpost of the North Korean nuclear weapons programme, I was dying for a pee and my mind was spent. I'm fairly certain the scientists working for dictators on actual nuclear weaponry sprinkle amphetamines on their porridge to make sure they remain focussed on that shit for an entire day - clearly mugs like me relying on the sugar rush from a bowl of Coco Pops in the morning were just pretenders. Taking a break and heading upstairs to the toilet my brain did its usual thing and fully embraced the microsleep - disengaged from the rest of my body, let my limbs slip into cruise control, and with it allowed me to career head-on into unbridled shame.

Standing there relieving several hours' worth of coffee consumption (that Coco Pops rush was short-lived and I needed another boost to keep my eyes open), I was blissfully staring into space when I started to suspect something wasn't quite right. My brain slowly started to emerge from the fog and cycled through the initial questions used by bleary-eyed interns the world over to determine what wasn't quite right. Did I put clean underwear on this morning? Check. Did I lock the front door? Check. Am I in the right office? Check. Hmmm, well that was the basics covered but I still wasn't sure what it could be... Well, I thought, if I've got clean underwear on, the house isn't about to be burgled and I've turned up to the right place, it surely can't be anything important.

My brain started to drift back into blissful ignorance when it struck me – dawning on me like a key piece of evidence being revealed to a detective trying to solve a case, my ears picked up on the fact there was something distinctly wrong with the audio of the situation… Now for those of you not familiar with using a urinal (be you a member of the fairer sex, or one of those guys who likes to enjoy the quite frankly bizarre ritual of a sit-down wee), there's typically barely any noise registered - it's like a silencer has been fitted to a gentleman's member and he becomes a pissing ninja. This is distinctly unlike using a toilet where most of us seem to enjoy making it sound like we've opened a portal to the base of Niagara Falls.

Oh no, this was very different to both of those. It was tinny. Hollow, almost thudding. Yep, that's definitely not right, I thought. My brain kicked into life, angrily emerging from its slumber like a Dad woken from his afternoon nap by the kids fighting upstairs. It didn't take long once it had disengaged from cruise control to help me realise what the hell was going on – sure I was peeing, and sure I was peeing in something white, but sweet mother Mary in my half-awake state I'd only gone and mistaken the paper towel bin for the urinal... the bloody paper towel bin!

Freaking out, and realising I obviously needed to stop peeing in the bin, I tried to stop but I'll tell you what - the ability to stop peeing and not crumble under the pressure that immediately builds inside is a skill reserved purely for monks and endurance athletes.

It should come as no surprise to learn that I am neither.

I simply couldn't stop peeing - the ship had long sailed on that one - but that didn't stop me in my panic from trying to step from the bin to the urinal. Not a smart move, not a smart move at all. "Shit, shit, shit," I murmured as I consequently laid waste to the beautifully decorated wall of the mens' toilet, peeing across its entire length all the way to the urinal. By the time I reached it, I'd finished. Typical.

Fearing someone would come in at any moment and catch me in my moment of madness, I zipped up, washed up and bolted out of there like I'd just done a smash and grab raid in Hatton Garden.

I quickly resumed my position in the lab and tried to avoid drawing suspicion to myself, but I was a nervous wreck. I was constantly looking through the windows, half expecting a mob of cleaners to be advancing down the corridor to haul me off for a beating. I've not been that stressed over possibly being confronted over something shameful since I got caught with porn in school and the Head Teacher played a game of 'will I or won't I tell your parents?'. Nice work Miss Kirkby - I'm fairly certain you took five years off my life expectancy with all the stress I endured from that shit.

Several days later I had still managed to avoid being caught by the cleaning Gestapo and was relieved to find that they hadn't started to revolt after being unable to find a culprit. There was never any mention of the degenerate who had violated the poor waste paper towel bin, and so it appeared that my shame would remain hidden forevermore. But, in a clichéd blunder seen in many a movie, this was only until I got drunk enough to tell my colleagues, and then somehow word got back to the cleaners, who proceeded to scowl at me every time they saw me, culminating in one gesturing resentfully to me one day across the car park - the jury's out as to whether they were merely scratching their neck or giving me the old throat-slicing threat so often seen in gangland feuds, but I think we all know which one it really was.

I started looking for a new job that evening.

Faux pas 2

The hand dryer

Not long after that I did indeed manage to find another job and ended up moving a few hundred miles to live with my girlfriend. It was all part of an attempt to become slightly more grown up and independent, and ultimately "a catch". You see, the writing was on the wall - no longer would the man-child whose parents made his lunch, was unable to drive and still rocked Wallace & Gromit bedsheets be able to keep hold of this stunning example of the finer sex. She was working at a FTSE 100 company surrounded by wealthy, successful guys who were able to enjoy the finer things in life, and so I clearly had to step up in every way. Not only was she far better in every way than me (prompting me to happily smile and nod along in agreement when people would see us and claim I was punching well above my weight) but she was 100% capable of giving me an absolute beating and I can't explain why, but that really did it for me, too. Thinking about it, there might have been a smidge of Stockholm Syndrome at play… Anyway, needing a new job to show I was capable of doing more than just dressing myself, I took up a position in the high-risk high-reward world of sales.

It was a completely different arena for me – no longer could I shuffle into work in a crumpled shirt, my brain still asleep but my body seemingly going through the motions of working. Oh no, there was absolutely zero room for micro-sleeping corporate zombies - it was a place where people were suntanned to within an inch of their life, where pink shirts and fast cars were de rigueur, and where energy levels never dropped below 98% thanks to a heady mix of caffeine, sugar and bonus-seeking enthusiasm.

Standing up and being counted was the name of the game, and making good impressions was a key part of it. Unsurprisingly, it took me a bit of time to adjust to this having come from the world of science where making an effort was deemed to be combing your hair and hanging a shirt up before wearing it, never mind ironing the damn thing. Pretty soon I was skating on thin ice, with it being touch and go who would hit their target first - me and my sales number on the wallchart, or the Directors and the P45 bullseye on my back. So when a new Managing Director joined the company I decided it was my time to shine, turn over a new leaf and finally start getting somewhere.

The first week of his tenure went past without him even visiting the office once. Damn. That was five days of wasted effort - I'd pulled out all the stops and even gone to the trouble of ironing the sleeves of my shirts, even though they'd be hidden under my suit jacket – the sleeves for fuck's sake! Well sod that, I thought, I'll ease off the daily efforts to impress and knock it out the park on the day he finally does turn up.

Over the weekend though, my car rather unhelpfully decided to bow out after several years of loyal service (taking with it a good chunk of my bank balance), which forced me to take the train to work for the foreseeable future and walk at least 25 minutes from the station to my office each day. No problem, I thought, I'll enjoy the walk through the leafy rural streets to the office.

Monday morning came, and with it, a monsoon of Indian

proportions. Shit. No problem, I've got a raincoat, I thought as I got ready to leave the house. Now something I'd not really considered was that it's fine having a waterproof jacket as the water will just run off and leave you dry, but where does the water go? Gravity is a cruel bitch, and so unless you've been savvy enough to nab yourself a pair of waterproof trousers to go with that jacket, a la trainspotter or mountain hiker, your investment in a waterproof jacket is about as useful as a cotton condom. By the time I realised, though, it was too late - they were soaked through.

Rocking up to the office after traipsing through the monsoon I was greeted by a colleague. "Morning Tom - hey, have you got yourself a new suit?" they asked. I just stared at them - I didn't dare take off my raincoat as it would reveal a wonderfully 80s two-tone grey suit. Of course I wasn't paying homage to that wonderful decade. Oh no, my trousers were simply soaked through with bastard rainwater turning them almost black whilst my bone dry jacket was the lightest of greys.

Clearly I couldn't keep my raincoat on all day, nor sit in sodden trousers, and it was ridiculous to even think about heading home to get changed as that would have been a three hour round trip. Fancying myself as some kind of corporate Bear Grylls, I decided to head into the toilets and try to fashion some kind of drying contraption. Locking myself in a cubicle I tried to pat my trousers dry with great big wads of toilet paper. This achieved a grand total of fuck all, yet left my legs completely covered in small chunks of white fluff. Shit. Venturing out of the cubicle I tried to remove the specks of toilet roll by soaking a paper towel in warm water and rubbing my legs with that. This had the grand result of actually smearing the tissue paper into my trousers and making it look like... well, you can imagine what a pair of trousers with a smeared white stain across the crotch looks like. Plus it managed to add even more water to the mix, which was the exact opposite of what I was trying to achieve from rubbing them with the paper in the first place. Bollocks... back to square one again.

And then, in a moment of clarity, it struck me – the hand dryer. Yes, the hand dryer! If I could dry them on the hand dryer they'd not only be dry but I could then easily brush off the smeared-on flecks of toilet paper and not look like I'd disappeared to the toilet for the last 10 minutes for a cheeky *tommy tank*.

Hypothetically the plan was sound. Logistically, it was anything but – trying to get my trousers close enough to the damn thing was proving to be a nightmare. It took several attempts to crack it.

Attempt number 1: the ballet leg extension. This crafty little manoeuvre had me shaking and sweating as I strained to keep my outstretched leg under the hand dryer, all the while trying not to slip on the wet tiled floor and crumple to the ground. This really wasn't helped by the fact it took me a good four or five attempts each time to get my leg up, leaving me with barely any time for drying before the machine stopped and I had to push the button to start my sweating, shaking ballet routine all over again. Giving up, I quickly moved onto a different approach.

Attempt number 2: the tiptoe and thrust technique. This wasn't my finest hour and I was really hoping that nobody was going to walk in, because if they did, they would have found me trying to stand on my tiptoes and thrusting my crotch up towards the hand dryer... The sad thing is, I can't strain like that without frowning and biting my lip like some kind of 80s pornstar, which would have been made all the more harrowing for anyone that would have walked in by the fact that at one point my crotch got a little too close, forcing me to let out a high-pitched yelp quickly followed by a low-pitch groan. These were all the sex noises you'd expect from a couple engaged in the art of lovemaking, yet they were coming from a single man. A man with his crotch stuffed against the vent of a hand dryer, no less.

Realising it was going nowhere and that people would start asking questions about what I was up to and if I was alright (which in turn would rapidly reduce the odds of someone walking in), I decided to go for the direct solution – whipping the trousers off and just holding them under the dryer.

And that was where I began attempt number 3: the standing-in-your-pants-and-drying-them-by-hand technique. I've never known fear like it. There's a particular amount of uncertainty that comes with standing in your pants in the office toilets, casually drying your trousers under the hand dryer: namely, what the hell will happen if someone walks in and sees me like this? I mean it's not the kind of fear you'd get from dropping the soap in a prison shower and wondering what will happen next, but hey, first world problems are still worth worrying about.

The drying was going well. Really well. I'd nearly done it, I'd nearly dried the bloody things. There was just one ankle left to finish. I was feeling pretty smug. So much so I let out a little chuckle and nodded at myself in the mirror, muttering "Well done you savvy bastard, you've turned this right round." And then it happened... that's when my smugness packed up and ran off, leaving me like a rabbit in the headlights.

Someone walked in. It was only the new MD! Shit. Best make that a rabbit with myxomatosis in the headlights of a Ferrari.

It was like a scene in a movie where a gang member drives past a rival in slow motion and they stare at one another with a look of disbelief on their face before all hell breaks loose. But we were not in LA, and neither I nor my new MD were hustling for the Bloods or the Cripps. We were in the Royal Borough of Berkshire, and so whilst there was the rabbit in the headlights stare from me as I stood and held my trousers close to me (clutching them tightly as I tried to cover my Bart Simpson pants), and a look of sheer disbelief from the MD, there was no ensuing chaos, no firing (literal or otherwise) and thankfully not a single word spoken... just a frown. A frown like no other frown I'd had thrown my way up to then or since - it was so powerful it made me doubt several of my life choices. And so petrified by fear, and with a good helping of shame, I simply stood there and held my trousers to my chest and waited for him to pee, wash his hands, dry them on the motherfucker of a hand dryer and leave. I'm pretty sure I closed my eyes at one point, like a scared child hoping that if it doesn't see the monster it won't see them and tear them to pieces.

As he pulled open the door to leave he paused and, without turning to acknowledge me, let out a simple yet telling

"Hmmm". The new MD was a man of few words, and I would later learn that his "Hmmm" was in actual fact his way of saying "Your days are numbered you complete fuckwit."

Sadly, this wouldn't be the last embarrassing incident with the new MD in a toilet…

Faux pas 3

Synchronicity

Surviving the trouser-drying incident was a relief, and managing to go several weeks without the new MD making any mention of it was a miracle. All seemed to be going well - the company was growing, the MD was able to report large profits, and I was yet to be fired for my quite frankly appalling sales figures.

Thankfully the MD and I had managed to avoid bumping into each other in the toilet too, which was a relief. I'm rubbish at making small talk at the best of times, let alone trying to do it in a toilet with the memory of that debacle clouding my thoughts. But then the most peculiar thing started to happen. Not only did we find ourselves in the toilet at the same time, but unbelievably we started to synchronise our toilet breaks...

It was a hot summer and we worked in a lovely little office which looked great but had the thermal properties of a greenhouse and all the ventilation of a bank vault, so everyone was downing glasses of water on top of the copious amounts of coffee and RedBull needed to maintain the energy levels needed for sales. It was only a matter of time before two people's toilet visits synced. I was just unlucky enough to do it with the MD. Oh, and did I mention that there were only two urinals so there was no way to avoid being right next to him?

Here's a little summary of our toilet visits.

Visit number 1: no acknowledgement from either of us.

Visit number 2: a raised eyebrow from the MD.

Visit number 3: a nod and a pursing of the lips to indicate "I've realised we're synchronised and it's damn weird."

Visit number 4: I couldn't resist. I had to say something, anything, to break the awkwardness. But I panicked just before speaking, worrying that what I was about to say would seem weird, and then the flashbacks of the trouser incident started to muddle my thoughts, which all culminated in me blurting out - as he was stood next to me at the urinal in full flow - "Erm, I could hold it in for you, if you'd like?"

There really is no good time to say that sentence, definitely not when standing right next to another man at the urinals, and especially not when that man is your MD. In my panic I wanted to appear to be helpful and thought that offering to break the synchronisation of our toilet stops would be a really thoughtful gesture. I just remember turning to see if he was happy with my suggestion, and so there I was, stood facing my MD, having just propositioned him in the weirdest way possible, smiling and seeking his approval, all the while with my penis still hanging out. There are no words I can use to describe the awkwardness... What if he misheard me, even just a little? What if he heard me proposition him with "I could hold it for you, if you'd like?" Frankly, I count myself lucky not to have gotten a visit from the local constabulary.

I have no idea what he said to me, I can't even remember what expression he had on his face. I think I blacked out.

Your brain does that with traumatic incidents.

It's little wonder that after that my interactions with the MD dwindled to just a few times a year, always when there were others around, and often with a significant distance between us. Come to think of it, my MD was displaying the same sort of techniques needed when having to deal with someone who had indecently exposed themselves. Oh god, he definitely thought I was an unhinged pervert.

I mean, if the shoe fits…

Faux pas 4

Know your brands

It will come as no great surprise to learn that I didn't last long in that sales role.

Realising that I just couldn't hack the high-pressure sales culture, I instead sought out a role in a company that would allow to me work at a more leisurely pace, and not feel compelled to wear skinny-fit suits or have the continuous energy levels of a kid with ADHD who's living off Red Bull.

And so I began working for one of the biggest engineering firms in the country.

Ah yes, engineering - a heady mix of grey suits, grey hair, and grey equipment. It was a place where you could find 25 year old engineers who had the same social skills, dress sense and energy levels as the 65 year olds. I had finally found my home!

It was with sure-fire certainty that I felt I could fly under the radar there, revert back into my beloved corporate zombie mode of brain-asleep-yet-body-seemingly-functioning, and emerge at the end of a long career with a healthy pension and a well-rested mind, body and soul.

Whilst I initially joined a team led by a wonderfully kind man who had the contacts and respect of the entire industry like some kind of engineering Mafia godfather, I soon ended up being forced to join a team led by a straight-laced engineer called Malcolm. He was a real company man - following the absolute letter of each and every policy, he lived and breathed the company, making us all suspect that if he was to cut himself he would bleed the colours of the logo.

My plan of an easy life went to shit in about five days.

Malcolm didn't give any indication he was anything other than the personification of beige, until it came to Fridays. Fridays were dress down day in this company, and whilst normally in any other company that would mean staff revealing their true colours of being aligned to one of the fashion subclasses such as goth, geek, exhibitionist or poser, in an engineering company that meant more of the same – grey shirts, grey trousers and grey jumpers.

On my first Friday in his team Malcolm waltzed in to the office looking like he was straight out of the FatFace catalogue – Converse trainers, slim fit jeans, flowery shirt with sleeves rolled up and a navy blue gilet. I couldn't believe my eyes. We had ourselves a real-life Clark Kent! I was impressed, and decided I was going to tell him how impressed I was that he's a savvy dresser, a) to be nice, and b) to try and curry some favour with my new boss.

That morning we had to drive to another office and I ended up car sharing with him. After a few minutes of chit-chat I jumped straight to it. "Do you know what Malcolm? I think you look like a FatFace model." His eyebrows furrowed and he turned his head slightly towards me. "Sorry, what did you say?" Hmmm, maybe he didn't hear me. Time to up the enthusiasm and volume. "You look like a FatFace model!" I bellowed, with my best beaming smile spread across my face. His face, however, did not reciprocate the smile. Oh no, in fact his face was incredulous... "I beg your pardon?!" he barked at me. Oh shit. Something was wrong. Something was very wrong. Maybe his clothes were from M&S and I'd insulted his choice of retailer, or he had some weird personal hatred of FatFace.

No, that wasn't it at all. Then it dawned on me as his face went red and he clenched his jaw in anger.

He had absolutely no idea there was a brand called FatFace. None at all. And so in that moment my boss went from thinking I was a reasonably nice new member of his team to thinking I was an absolute arsehole who clearly didn't give a shit, and wanted to tell him to his face that I thought said face was chunkier than Kim Kardashian's arse.

Marvellous, just marvellous.

Even after my frantic attempts to tell him about the brand he still didn't believe me and so what followed was a very awkward and quiet drive to the meeting, similar to every car trip I take with my mother in law. By the following week, however, he seemed to be okay about it all, so I can only imagine he'd Googled it and realised that I simply wasn't good with words sometimes, and not actually a complete dick who liked to insult people in enclosed spaces.

I never did see him wear the gilet again though...

Faux pas 5

Caption time

Things seemed to settle down following that little misunderstanding, and after a while I had a period of time seconded to the Media team. With it came the responsibility for photographing my colleagues at events and other outings, before posting the images alongside articles and press releases on both internal and external websites.

I fully embraced the role, envisioning myself as some kind of Milan fashion photographer crossed with a wartime correspondent. Swanning into a drab meeting room where the air was stale and thick with the odour of armpits and Lynx Africa (the engineer's aroma of choice) I realised I needed to tone it down a bit as I wouldn't last much longer wearing sunglasses indoors with chinos, a pink shirt and a tripod slung over my shoulder whilst chewing gum in that classic 'I couldn't care less about any of you' way that most teenagers and people from London tend to do.

The role was fun, and a particular highlight was sharing some of the images not suitable for publishing with a select few colleagues and offering up captions to elicit some chuckles on an otherwise boring day.

Now, knowing that company emails are monitored (I always imagined there was a team of company intelligence officers in the basement, trawling through thousands of messages each day, ready to drag unsuspecting employees into a darkened meeting room for a beating, like the Stasi of East Germany back in the day) I kept it relatively PC. I also thought by only sharing them with my closest colleagues, aka the friends I could trust, there was no risk of me being hauled in front of HR and asked to explain why I was sharing photos of David with his hands out in front of him, nearly touching and a very solemn expression on his face with the caption "David finally confessed to the size of his micro penis."

Being a nice guy though, I always wanted to make people in the team feel included and be in on any jokes, and so I couldn't help but think about Peter who I knew was sat between two of the guys I would be sending this to and so would inevitably hear and see what was going on and might feel disappointed he wasn't involved. Having been that kid growing up who wasn't part of the 'in-crowd' (my acne, glasses and quite incredible monk-like haircut made sure of that) and therefore rarely included in jokes and escapades, I was determined not to let Peter feel like that.

So I copied him in.

Thanks to me being more snap-happy with the camera than a Japanese tourist there was a hearty bundle of photos and captions in the email - from Steven presenting at a conference with a very surprised look on his face as he leant on the lectern and the associated caption referring to his prostate exam no doubt taking place and being the cause of his expression, to Grant's horrendous two-tone shiny shoes and a quip about the fact he should have gone to Specsavers. Like I said, all relatively PC - the closest I thought it got to being frowned upon by anyone outside the group was another photo of Steven, this time with his arms out wide in front of him as he was showing the attendees how big a device was. But of course that's boring as hell, so the caption instead suggested he was showing people the size of his last one-night stand's knickers. Immature? Yes. Funny? Barely. Funny when you know that his last one-night stand's knickers were actually twice as large as that? Absolutely.

Out the email went, and I sat back, relaxed and awaited the exchange of emails and banter that normally followed. But on this occasion I instead heard sharp intakes of breath at desks around me, and saw people wincing. Oh no. That wasn't meant to happen. I turned around and gingerly asked one of the people on the distribution list what it was that people were thinking was so controversial. "You sent it to Peter," they replied, as if that was enough for me to realise my mistake. "So?" I queried. "Well, you know, Peter's got a daughter..." they trailed off. "Yes, AND?!" I demanded, getting more than a little impatient. "Well she's got Down's Syndrome…" Ah. Right. Well, that was indeed a bit of a problem.

You see, I had also included a photo of Tom presenting, and Tom's style was very animated - he would gesticulate like he'd had seven pints and was playing in the charades world championships. Trying to photograph him without him looking like an utter mess was nigh on impossible. So, having only unusable photos of Tom, I included the most absurd one in the email, where he resembled someone who was severely handicapped (I feel awful writing that but it's the only way to explain…). Underneath I wrote the caption "We are proud to be an equal opportunities employer!"

I felt like a complete bastard.

It turns out Peter thought I was a complete bastard, too.

Most of the people on the distribution list did as well, especially as I'd been on a diversity training course only a few months before, where Peter had actually explained to the group that his daughter was severely handicapped and shared some of the insensitivities they'd faced in light of it...

There's not many times when people's faces actually manage to pull the same expression as emojis, but at that moment in time mine perfectly matched the grimacing, teeth exposed emoji as I felt genuine remorse at the situation I found myself in. Not since I'd accidentally shat myself in the local swimming pool had I felt this emotion (I'd like to point out I was only 10 years old at the time which is kind of like mitigating circumstances, although I must also admit I just waded out the pool without looking back, leaving that ticking time bomb to be discovered and the entire pool to be shut, which immediately wipes out any grace I get for being a mere child. This is regret number 174 in my life).

I knew saying that "I'm really sorry but I have this thing where I'm present but not present, like a bit of a zombie, and that's why I didn't remember your story about your daughter," wouldn't cut it by way of an apology. But I threw it out there anyway just to test the waters. It was met with such hostility that I was fairly sure HR, the press and the local lynching mob were about to be made aware of my faux pas.

But in the end, HR didn't haul me in for another disciplinary, the local newspaper didn't run an article on the insensitive bastard of Wiltshire, and no mobs of angry locals tried to drag me kicking and screaming from the safety of my desk to the Town Hall for a good old fashioned beating. Surprisingly it turned out Peter was okay with it, although I think that was more down to my grovelling apology and the contribution I made to the charity bike ride he was about to undertake for the local Down's Syndrome charity. Nothing like buying your way out of guilt…

For anyone that thinks this is bullshit and you can't buy favours, forgiveness, or freedom from guilt, just consider the last time you bought your other half flowers or a nice bottle of wine, treated them to a nice meal out, or organised a little trip away… Yeah, exactly - whatever the journey, they pretty much all reach the same intended destination of smiles, solidarity and if you're really cooking on gas, sex.

On that last point, it recently dawned on me that unless you're in the sweet spot of the 'honeymoon period' of a relationship, getting laid is most likely going to cost you. First few dates? Taxis, meals and drinks are the name of the game. Married? All that plus more. Married with kids? Same again, except now with the added penalty of babysitting fees and the excitement of not knowing if all the effort will actually lead to sex or at least one of you just passing out with exhaustion. But here's a real conundrum - whilst I'm always keen to enjoy a cheeky foray into the bedroom, I'm tighter than a duck's arse (yet another phrase which terrifies me to think of how it came about). Sadly I'm also very accomplished in annoying my wife which means I stand precisely zero chance of getting lucky purely based on gallantry, chivalry and general husbandry, and ergo am forced to engage in the aforementioned costly act which I'm sure we can all agree is basically marital prostitution.

And that single sentence alone will provide the only check I'll ever need to tell if my wife actually reads this, because she sure as shit won't let me get away with writing stuff like that without at least a few choice words being thrown my way!

Faux pas 6

Interview propositioning

I began thinking that perhaps it was best if I moved into a different team and cut short my secondment to the Media team. I began thinking if I can't be trusted with internal emails, I probably shouldn't be trusted with the social media accounts of one of the biggest engineering firms in the country.

By 'I' I mean 'management', and by 'began thinking' I mean 'decided'. Fun times.

With it being such a large company there were lots of opportunities to transfer to other roles, and thankfully the one I wanted was actually in the department I was already part of. The trouble was, it needed me to interview for it. Now I've got no problem with sitting and answering probing questions, building some light-hearted camaraderie and doing all the things you need to emerge successfully out the other side. It's a lot like being brought in for questioning by the Police. Or so I've been told... The problem is my inability to maintain 100% focus. I can do 90% no problem, 95% after an extra-strong coffee, and 99% if there's the fear of being made homeless as a result of not getting the job. But never quite 100%. No, that magical, mythical percentage of focus it appears is permanently out my reach, and boy does my brain like to concentrate all of its 'fuck-things-up-ability' into that remaining 1%...

The interview was all set. It was a 4pm interview, which

wasn't ideal as it was late in the day and there was a risk I would barely strike out at a 90% focus rate, let alone the ideal 99%, but I had faith that a double espresso at 3:45pm would help me sail through with no problems whatsoever. The big day finally came, and I was ready. The only problem was that I had a day full of meetings, calls and documents that needed producing before 4pm. With a steely focus in my mind, I fired up my laptop at 9am and got down to business, furiously typing away like a court reporter jacked up on speed.

The day was a flurry of activity as expected. I looked up at the clock on the wall. It smugly revealed its hands to show it was 3:56pm. Oh shit. Where the hell did the day go? What room was the interview in? How long would it take me to get there? What about the double espresso I needed to keep me focused?! No, no, no, no – my plan of being prepared had fallen apart like a cheap watch… without that coffee I was a mere mortal, my regular corporate zombie self, ready to hit the self-destruct button on my career at any point.

Sat there with a blank expression on my face and staring into the distance I was almost ready to jack it all in and give up before I'd even started. But then I remembered how much I hated sitting next to Eric and so I thought sod it, it's now or never, let's do this! And so with that I set off with a cavalier can-do attitude and spring in my step, ready to smash the interview and move on to pastures new.

Thankfully I made it in time and the interview was going amazingly well. The fact I was saying that in my mind after only four minutes wasn't an issue. I'm all for the tortoise and the hare approach to life, but I bet the hare was absolutely loving it whilst the going was good! So why not enjoy it whilst things are going well? By the 15 minute mark we started to really get down to business, and the hiring manager told me "I'm looking for someone who can blow my socks off or do something really amazing. But obviously above board and legal!" Cue laughter all round. Buoyed by the sense of joviality he'd thrown out, my brain clocked out - hitting the autopilot button, it packed up and went for a cheeky tea break, leaving my mouth to free-wheel. You can safely assume nothing good ever comes from that.

"That's a shame," I replied, grinning and suggestively lifting my eyebrows whilst looking at him as I lined up the punchline, "because if you gave me the job I'd blow more than just your socks off!" I started laughing even louder than before, like when you're joking with friends and you start one-upping each other. But there was a problem. He had stopped laughing. In fact he was just staring at me. He was waiting for me to stop laughing at my own joke, and realise I'd just joked about giving him a blowjob in return for the job… and at that point it dawned on me, and my brain re-entered the room, like an unsuspecting audience member at a Derren Brown show who's just gyrated like a stripper on stage in front of hundreds of people.

Shit.

I quickly started thinking how to salvage the situation. What were the options? Jump out the window and run into the distance? No, it's only the first floor but I've got glass ankles, they'd never survive the drop. Try to fake a meltdown and hope to get the incident written off as part of the whole 'episode' I was having? No, I'd not only not get the job, I'd lose any chance of getting another job in the team. Plus I wasn't very good at amateur dramatics. Nope, the answer was simple - damage limitation. And so with only seconds remaining of this awkward silence before it was completely unsalvageable, I did the only thing I could muster in such a short space of time, with panic clawing at my rationale – I smiled. A great big cheesy smile, with my eyebrows slowly raising up higher and higher. What I was going for was the look a small child gives you when you find out they've done something wrong and they try to play it all cute. But I was 32 years old, and so all I achieved was a seedy look that reinforced the idea of it being a proposition and screamed "So how about it, big boy?"

The atmosphere after that was pretty frosty. Not just frosty, it was fully-blown Arctic. Despite there being more interviews the following day, the manager called me up about half an hour later and told me I had been unsuccessful in my application. Ah. I'm not sure why, but I was hoping there might have still been a tiny chance he'd come to see the funny side of it.

The judging and distrust from that manager lasted some time, including an incident when we were in a team meeting about recognising sexual harassment in the workplace and he looked at me across the room, causing me to look away, laugh and blurt out "Oh fuck off!" under my breath - which then led to everyone in the room who wasn't aware of this underlying situation thinking I was just a pent up sex pest who thought the concept of reporting sexual harassment was absurd. Brilliant.

I'd like to say that's the only time one of my interviews

nosedived... however there have (unsurprisingly) been quite a few. One notable incident came after I'd successfully passed the paper-sift stage for a job at The Atomic Weapons Establishment. Now this is the organisation responsible for the design and manufacture of the warheads for the UK's nuclear missile arsenal. The security clearance papers alone were nearly 70 pages long! So it was no mean feat to even get that far, and I was determined to be an ideal candidate and hopefully beat the other applicants to the job.

At the time I was without a car (I still had the heap of shit that caused the wet trouser debacle), and so had to get my girlfriend to drive me to the secure site for my interview. Gingerly making my way inside the reception block I was disappointed to find that despite its top secret nature the security was on a par with Midlands Airport. I was expecting some kind of walk-through x-ray machine like in Total Recall, but instead I was simply given a visitor's badge and asked to wait for the interviewer to come get me. All grand ideas of being the next Q to the nuclear arms race's Bond rapidly disappeared.

Eventually a tall, thin, unassuming man (think a nerdy Stephen Merchant. Actually, just think of Stephen Merchant) met me and took me through a series of corridors until we entered a small nondescript room. The decor was hardcore 70s and there was even a solitary plant slowly dying in the corner. Classic secretive military site.

Also in the room was a beautiful lady who was part of the management team in the area I was trying to join. Whilst she too dressed in the same nondescript office attire as their resident Stephen Merchant doppelganger, there was one key difference - she had undone quite a few buttons on her shirt. And peeking out through the opening of her shirt was the most gloriously perfect cleavage I could ever wish for.

It was a test. It had to be.

I knew my mission - answer all their questions and avoid staring at her cleavage. With a potentially life-changing career on the line and the fact I'd been seeing breasts for over 15 years thanks to stumbling across porn before I was even 10 years old, you'd have thought it would've been a piece of piss. But remember my unachievable 100% concentration level and all the 'fuck-things-up-ability' that takes place in the remaining 1% after I max out at 99%? Well, all it took was for me to stumble on a question of "Can you tell us the difference between accuracy and precision?" (I still don't know the answer) and whilst thinking I found my eyes inadvertently drawn to *the place that shall not be looked at*. Suddenly I couldn't even remember what the question was as it dawned on me that I'd been staring at her chest for some time and then to my horror as I raised my eyes up my gaze met with hers, and I felt decidedly sheepish as I watched her shift uncomfortably in her seat and try to pull her shirt closed. Fuck it, she'd caught me good and proper.

To make matters worse, I got clocked another three times before the interview ended… and to truly consign myself to the 'do not hire or even interview again' pile, I rounded the interview off with a ridiculous question. You know when they ask you if you have any questions for them? They're undoubtedly giving you the chance to quiz them about pensions and growth opportunities. To ask, at 11am, where the nearest pub is, is definitely not what they had in mind. I genuinely didn't see the problem with asking that or the need to give context, because it was the only landmark my friend (who was picking me up) knew and his instructions of "I'll pick you up at the pub around the corner at 11:30," were suitably vague on the actual location of said pub and so I needed some help with that. But to them it was the final nail in the coffin of that disastrous interview. I'm pretty sure they felt they could hire a pervert if push came to shove. They could also probably hire an alcoholic. But an alcoholic pervert? Too far.

Having worked with one for a few years, I can safely say that's sound logic - otherwise the Pandora's box of HR gets opened up and no amount of training can sort that kind of shit-show out.

Faux pas 7

Putting the D in BBC

When my secondment to the Media team was over I was unceremoniously returned to my original team, who welcomed me back not so much with open arms, but more the kind of begrudging *we don't really give a shit but we're British so we'll smile and be polite* way that the nation gives every sports team returning from a failed attempt to win something abroad.

Like those sports teams, I shuffled past, nodding, smiling, throwing out the odd grimace, and hoping nobody would give me too much grief for at least the first day I was back. And like those sports teams, I had to get stuck back into the same old routines, preparing for the next challenge. Not necessarily because I wanted to, but because it put money in my pocket and allowed me to live a life outside of the world of work - although as that world seemed to occupy every waking minute that just left sleep. Maybe that's why I once went and spent more money on a mattress than I did on my first car. I felt like such a baller.

On that particular occasion I remember being stood in the showroom with my girlfriend and she told me how much the bed we were checking out cost. I was glad it had such a thick memory foam topper because it broke my fall perfectly as the shock took hold and caused my legs to buckle from beneath me. Steadying myself, I looked around at the setup in the beautifully crafted area that resembled one of those immaculate and oh-so-grown-up bedrooms you see in the property pages of a high-end magazine... I looked at the beautiful walnut bed frame, the matching bedside tables, chest of drawers and gigantic wardrobe and thought that it wasn't bad value at all if we were going to have it for 10 years and live like we're suave lawyers in central London. So I turned to her, smiled, and said "Okay, let's get the lot, let's go wild!" At which point she gave me the look, the look of mockery she'd give someone who's just replied "Why The Face?" when asked to explain the acronym WTF, and she told me that the price was just for the mattress. Just the mattress... All I remember after that is signing a finance agreement and then projectile vomiting out the car window on the drive home. At the time we thought I'd gotten a stomach bug, but looking back I think it was the shock of spending more money on some springs and fabric than I'd spent on Paulo, my beloved VW Polo.

Anyway, eventually I began to make good progress in the team again, helping deliver some great results on a project which made headlines with its findings, and at one point I was asked by a member of the Corporate Affairs team to represent the company in an interview with the local BBC Radio station. I didn't care if it wasn't actually because of my performance in the team and it was just the fact that everyone else before me on the list they'd asked was unavailable. This was it – a chance to be on the BBC! Well, BBC Radio. Okay fine, in truth it was just BBC Radio Hertfordshire. But look, it doesn't matter how low down the ladder it was, I was ecstatic!

Clearly the guy from Corporate Affairs could tell I wasn't used to being interviewed by the media. I think the giveaway was when he asked me "Have you had any media engagement before?" to which I replied "A few years ago

I was interviewed by the local paper when I saw a swan walk into a shop." And so he hurriedly set up a session to brief me on the ins and outs of this line of work, what to aim for, what to avoid, and generally how to make sure my five minutes on local radio didn't end up with the company being embroiled in some kind of scandal.

Piece of piss, I thought. From the look on his face when he turned up though, it was clear he felt it would be a far greater challenge. His face was so gloomy and forlorn, it looked like he had been tasked with defusing a nuclear warhead under the meeting room table. It soon became apparent why.

Running through the likely line of questioning from the radio show host, Mr Corporate Affairs soon began to run through them with pace as he saw that I was getting comfortable, understanding the direction he was wanting me to take and the glaring errors to avoid making.

"Make sure you stick to talking about the exciting development we've announced," he started, "and avoid answering any questions about our share price." I nodded enthusiastically. "In fact, try to avoid discussing anything other than the exact part of the business we're promoting. Oh and if they invite you to comment on the recent court case, try to say that it's not an area of the business you're involved with, and couldn't possibly comment for fear of not getting the facts right." Again, I nodded enthusiastically, trying to both convey the fact I wasn't completely useless as well as strike up a camaraderie with him to make it all a bit less formal.

Settling down and realising he didn't need to panic, he

relaxed, slouched back into his chair and said "Sorry, I don't mean to put words in your mouth," he said, laughing. Sensing a chance to push the camaraderie into overdrive I threw my head back and laughed hard, and that's when once again, my brain stepped out, my enthusiasm took over, and my burgeoning media career tanked faster than my attempts to chat up girls when I was a spotty bespectacled teenager.

"Well, as long as that's the only thing you'll try to put in my mouth!" I chortled. He looked at me. I mean properly looked at me. His laughter tailed off, the smile transitioning into a slightly open-mouthed grimace, and his eyes wincing as he processed the complete filth I'd just dolled out. Yep, that's right, Mr Corporate Affairs – this is the guy you're meant to be preparing to go on the radio and represent the company. No wonder he looked like he was deciding whether to cut the red wire or the blue wire on the nuke under the desk. Poor guy.

Surprisingly for us both, I was still able to do the interview (I really must have been the last name on the list), although on the way over to the station I was given the kind of instructions issued to an elderly relative asked to babysit for the first time – 'don't do this', 'make sure you do this' and even 'under no circumstances say this'. I still remember the last instruction written on the A4 crib sheet being written in capitals - 'DO NOT SWEAR'. Now I don't know if this was a standard line, or if he knew about my impressive potty mouth (growing up on a council estate and listening to some of the arguments that erupted, I was apparently quite adept at swearing by the age of 10, much to the dismay of my polite parents) but it ignited my mischievous streak. Heading into the studio he checked I understood all the instructions, and then he started to relax a little. Following a briefing from the BBC team on the format and expected etiquette I was ready to go. Just as I was about to enter the soundproofed room and warble into the ears of a few thousand listeners, I turned to Mr Corporate Affairs and exclaimed "Oh yeah, I almost forgot to say, as I tend to swear quite a bit I'd best release the pressure and get this lot out before I go on air," before releasing a torrent of swearing that would made even the most drunken of sailors take a sharp intake of breath in shock at the vulgarity and range of vocabulary used. Even I was impressed with one or two of them. Standing there, holding his clipboard, he blinked twice, swallowed, and looked at me with the expression of a man facing the firing squad. Thankfully neither of us had anything to worry about, and the interview went without a hitch, although it wasn't surprising to find that after that I wasn't invited to do any more media work. Bloody spoilsports!

Well, that is until years later when I was our company's rep on another flagship project where one of the companies leading it decided to make some promotional material to help raise awareness of all the good things it was doing.

Being a big international tech firm they quickly produced a PR plan, hired a film crew and set about doing interviews with the reps from each company. The aim was to get us all to wax lyrical about the project and what it would mean for the industry, and so we had to be prepared for a little Q&A in front of the camera to build up the footage they could then edit together into a slick promo clip to put out on social media.

Timescales were tight, and as I was in a fairly central

location the film crew decided they would film me to create our company's content. Despite having only a few days' notice I was fine with this - I'd recently had a haircut so wasn't looking too scruffy, my kids had both slept fairly well so I no longer resembled Gollum, and it was late summer so I actually had a bit of a tan for a change.

The day of filming came and I made my way into the office, excited for the new experience. There may have even been a bit of swagger in my step as I waltzed in. I made my way up to the top floor of the office where there was a frenzy of activity. It was quite fascinating seeing the PR people discussing angles and lighting with the film crew, and the hair and makeup people setting up their station ready to do any last minute tweaks to yours truly.

"Hi, I'm Tom, excited to meet you and be part of this little production!" I said, grinning and hoping my overly positive opening gambit would win them over. I didn't need to win anyone over, but for some reason I'd convinced myself they would be like most City slickers who wore shoes without socks and drank oat milk lattes, and treat everyone who lived outside the M25 with disdain.

"Lovely to meet you, I'm Felicity," the lead PR person smiled back, "come this way and we'll do a little run through before we start filming."

Taking me over to a little pair of armchairs next to a floor to ceiling window, the view was amazing thanks to how high up we were, and I was confident this would look amazing in the final footage.

"Hi Tom, I'm Madison and I'm going to guide you through

this today," came a voice from where the camera team was positioned. Ah, an American, I noted. In my eyes an extra layer of glamour was instantly in place since a bonafide media person was at the helm. An American. Settling down in the chair opposite me Madison began to explain how she would be sat off-camera and ask me to maintain eye contact with her and not the camera, and she wanted us to talk like we were having a conversation although it would be very much a Q&A style session.

"I'm sorry I'm going to have to ask you a lot of questions, some of them I'm sure you get asked a lot, and if you could keep the answers simple that would be great as I'm not an engineer," she said with a smile.

Nodding and smiling back I tried to put her at ease with "That's okay, don't worry about it, I've got two young kids and I'm used to them asking me stupid questions all day long, so go for it."

Her face grimaced and she shot back a terse "I'm not stupid," before looking down at her notes and taking a long slow breath and releasing through flared nostrils.

Bugger. Done it again, haven't I? I thought to myself.

After our dry run of the Q&A, which was carried out with such thinly veiled hatred for me that I thought she might well end up as my future wife, she wrapped up with "Okay, now just time for hair and makeup and we can start the real thing."

"Erm, do I really need it?" I foolishly asked.

With a look of pity as if talking to a sweet little child who asked a silly question, she smiled and looked me straight in the eyes before landing the knockout blow of "Oh hunny, you really do."

Fuck me... Americans, eh? Got to love their sass.

Trying to not let that jibe linger in my mind I was soon accosted by a lady who after a brief chat with Madison opened up a concertina-effect makeup case which contained all manner of lotions, potions and worryingly, glitter. I sincerely hoped she wasn't going to start throwing that shit about.

And so she got to work. After a light dusting of this and a little spray of that, I thought I was good to go. How wrong I was. Apparently a few good nights' sleep doesn't remove the effect of the previous three years of interrupted sleep. First she applied a cream to the bags under my eyes. Then she stood back, assessed the car crash of my face and went in for a second application. Standing back to admire her handiwork once more she tutted, frowned and came in for a third bite of the cherry. This time some kind of pen with a giant metal ball bearing on the end was being ground into my eye sockets.

"Argh, fuck, what's that for?!" I demanded to know.

"It's for the bags darling, you have children, no?" she asked.

"Yeah, two."

"Just two? My my my..." she muttered.

Feeling less and less confident about stepping out of the house, let alone in front of the camera, she was sure to deal me one last blow as she got out a hairbrush.

"Erm, you won't need that, I did my hair this morning," I told her.

"It's just needing a little tidy up," she said softly.

"But it wasn't even windy this morning!" I pleaded with her.

Oh well, I thought, people on TV end up with immaculately styled hair so I should trust her and let her do her thing and enjoy my well-groomed locks over the rest of the day.

With no chance to look in a mirror to see the transformation for myself, the camera and lights were fired up and it was go time. The next 10 minutes were full of me hamming it up with OTT smiles and hand gestures, whilst delivering my best corporate speak on how the project is revolutionary. Another few minutes of that and I'd have no doubt ended up with a nomination for a BAFTA!

"Okay, thank you Tom, I think we've got everything we need," said Madison.

"Oh wait, there's just the lookup shot left," interjected Felicity.

"The what?" I asked.

"You'll love it," she replied, "we're getting these great shots of everyone in the video where they're stood up but looking down at the ground, and as we move towards them with the camera they slowly raise their head until they're then looking directly at the camera."

"Okay, sure," I said, not sure at all if this was going to work or just make me look like a complete bellend.

And so with that we got to work. But in their never-ending desire for perfect lighting and background they decided that I should stand with my back to the floor to ceiling glass wall which lines the atrium which runs up the entire centre of our office building. This filled me with dread, because that meant I'd be visible to the hundreds of staff sat on all the other floors, who could watch me perform this absurd slow head raise move with a camera rushing towards me.

"Just one more, please Tom," the film team would say, "only this time try smiling as you raise your head up."

After seven takes the nightmare was over, and the small congregation of people on the other floors were able to stop watching and laughing at me and get back on with their jobs.

Needing the toilet I thanked them all and said my goodbyes. As I was washing my hands I looked in the mirror and recoiled in horror. It wasn't me looking back, it was some strange porcelain-white person with a side parting, like some kind of ventriloquist's dummy... and then it once again dawned on me - after inadvertently likening Madison's interview technique to a couple of annoying kids, she had had a little word with the hair and makeup lady and had clearly told her to do a number on me as revenge.

I was mortified. After an innocent slip of the tongue I was about to be immortalised in a PR campaign by a huge international tech company. I was hoping that because it was just on social media nobody in my team would see it.

A few weeks later the PR company excitedly emailed everyone advising them the final promotional clip was ready. Nervously I watched it, and my heart sank a little when I realised two things - firstly, that they had cut all but 10 seconds of my 10 minute interview, and secondly that I didn't look like a ventriloquist's dummy, but more of an embalmed choirboy. Oh, and those 'great' lookup shots? Mine was the only one out of the entire project team which wasn't used in the final video, which makes sense because the PR team provided us all with the individual footage in case we wanted to make our own promo clips. All I'll say is someone smiling whilst staring at the ground and then slowly raising their head up looks less like a Hollwood power shot and more like a manic serial killer standing over his latest victim and looking up at his next one. Horrendous stuff, and that's the reason why I permanently deleted that footage from our company's servers!

The final dagger in my heart came months later when it turned out that the PR company had sent the final clip to our marketing team for use at the big annual conference. I had no idea until I was stood on the stand we had paid for to promote our business, and some colleagues started to point and laugh at the TV screen. Turning to see what was so funny I was gutted to realise it was me. Seeing how crestfallen I looked, one of them came over and with a solemn look on his face and said to me "Mate, you look really ill in that video, are you alright?"

And that was pretty much the death knell for any hopes I had of having any involvement in PR for our company ever again!

Faux pas 8

It's all in the name

The benefits of being able to work for a big company like the engineering firm are that you can enjoy flexible working, and with it the opportunity to work from home when needed. The intentions are good, and commendable - designed to be a means of helping people struggling with child care, family dramas, healthcare appointments and those pesky visits for engineers to fix a faulty boiler/washing machine/mundane appliance that need you to be at home for the entire nine hour window they give you. However I'm fairly sure that most of the male employees under the age of 40 will at some point put it to use not for good but nefarious purposes, such as watching TV, wasting time on the internet, playing computer games, or the foundation of all working from home: watching porn. If you're male and under 40, try denying you've done one of those things whilst working from home. Yeah, I thought as much, you procrastinating dirt bags! And if your partner happens to be in that particular demographic, try quizzing them about their experiences of working from home - you'll love watching them squirm as they try to weasel their way out of telling you the truth.

One particular day I needed to work from home to make sure I was there to receive an online order that was due to be delivered, as opposed to having to come home in the dark after work and try to find it as the local delivery driver, who must surely have been training for the javelin event at the Olympics, was a fan of unceremoniously launching parcels over the fence and into the bushes.

The plan to work from home, however, hit a fairly major snag quite early on - I'd forgotten to bring my laptop back with me. Not fancying the mad dash to the office through rush hour traffic to then rush back home and no doubt find I'd missed the delivery, I decided to use my personal laptop and log in remotely. I hadn't used my laptop in quite a few years (mainly thanks to smut and social media being readily available via mobile phones) and so after waiting about two hours for it to boot up, I logged in. Whilst waiting for the company security checks to do their thing I decided to check out the files that were still saved on the old piece of junk. It's one of modern life's wonders, powering up a laptop that you've not used in a while. In the old days people would look at old photographs, scrapbooks and shoeboxes full of mementoes to retrace days gone by and reminisce about better times. In the age of digital technology, just turn on a device you've not used in a few years and it's a treasure-trove of memories, an absolute cornucopia of insights – the majority of which you probably won't be pleased to find, because they either confirm how boring your life has become or how badly you've aged. Like I said, a wonder of modern life.

Looking for a presentation I needed to reference in my emails later that day, I started looking through a folder full of them. And that's when I stumbled across one from my previous life in sales. Instantly I got flashbacks like a veteran reliving a terrifying moment from a conflict they'd served in. The atrocities were still fresh in my mind. I was clearly suffering from Post Traumatic Sales Disorder.

This particular presentation was from when I had been given a chance to step up into the big leagues and lead rather than being led. According to the Head of Sales, I needed to prepare a slide pack to brief all of the bosses on my plan for the new financial year at a sales retreat they'd organised.

This was it, I'd thought, the upper echelons of the sales world. I had envisaged it would be an intoxicating and decadent mix of luxury accommodation, free-flowing alcohol, semi-naked models and outrageous antics. If you've ever seen the Wolf of Wall Street movie, that's exactly what my mind had conjured up. Sadly, and rather expectedly, it was anything but that... the venue had seen better days long before we had got there, the alcohol was so expensive I daren't buy more than just one round for fear of poverty, and whilst we worked with some beautiful women, they only dressed like semi-naked models of the Victorian-era - a bit of ankle being on show was as risky as it got. To be fair, when half the team were young guys keen to get rich, die young and sleep with anything they could, and the other half were rich, miraculously still alive in their forties and tempted by anyone showing them more interest than their wives, you can understand why. But at the end of the day, it was still sales and so it was yet more good ol' days of high fives, pink shirts and a perpetual fear of my sales figures costing me my job, my home and my relationship. Oh how you've got to love sales...

Sat in my study at home all those years later I couldn't remember how the retreat had ended, nor even what I'd put forward to the bosses, so deciding to see what kind of drivel I presented back then I opened the presentation up, looked at the nonsense glaring at me and both laughed at my naivety and cringeworthy use of Clip Art. If you don't remember the original Clip Art, in all its clunky glory, then you're probably one of those kids who has never seen a tower PC or a floppy disc. Honestly, the youth of today... It was a special time to be alive, and the only way you wouldn't have used or seen the Clip Art of the duck about to smash a PC to smithereens with a mallet at least once a week is if you were doing a stretch in a remote Thai jail.

Figuring that was enough nostalgia for one day I closed the presentation down and was going to open the one I really needed when the phone rang. After finishing the call I returned to the laptop and saw that I'd left the cursor on the old sales retreat file in the list of presentations, and that something rather peculiar had happened – it had shown up the original title I'd saved it as, which was markedly different to one it had been saved as before it had been sent to the management team.

Seeing the original title, it dawned on me why things went south not long after I gave the presentation – you see whilst I'd sent it to them with a very generic title of 'Sales plan for Q1 to Q4', it would appear I was quite angry and bitter about the fact the stress of the job was crippling my social, romantic and financial situations.

"Hey Tom, you want to come to the pub for a night out?" my friends would ask.

"Sorry lads, I've got to work late to meet a deadline or I risk getting fired tomorrow," was a typical reply.

"Shall we go out for a nice meal tonight and grab a bottle of wine?" my girlfriend would suggest. "Definitely!" I'd say, before proceeding to ruin the romance by spending most of the meal lamenting the fact I'd not got any support and how in actual fact they'd hired another person to compete against me in a sales version of The Hunger Games.

Or occasionally there'd be the offer of "Do you fancy heading to London to watch the game and have a night out?" before I would have to inevitably let everyone down by saying "I'd love to, but because I'm shit at sales I haven't got enough money for my weekly shop let alone a mad weekend in the City."

It's funny, because it takes a certain type of person to either excel at (or merely survive) sales. Oh, and a good amount of luck. Angus, my Scottish colleague at the company had a fabulous sports car courtesy of a company just calling up one day and asking for a shed load of stuff, which he happened to be responsible for and subsequently earned him the ridiculous bonus he used to buy it. At the other end of the spectrum you can graft your absolute arse off and get nothing at all, as the enquiring company shafts you by eventually going with someone else or realises they can't afford it after all and cuts you off at the knees. I used to joke about scumbags selling their own Nan to make a bit of money, but I soon came to realise sales people were just as bad, and actually I could understand why - when you've got a mortgage, maybe even a family, and possibly even an unhealthy Haribo addiction (all eyes on you, Angus) you will do anything to avoid losing your only means of supporting those things and ending up on someone's sofa (or worse).

Yep, I think it's safe to say I'd reached my crisis point by that time the sales retreat came about. So it should come as no surprise to learn that at the point of creating it I had in fact initially saved it as 'Here's your sales retreat presentation you stupid wankers' before calming down and later renaming it with the generic title. Pretty witty I'd thought. I even afforded myself a little chuckle and said to myself "You whimsical bastard." Yet for some crazy reason despite it being renamed before I sent it across to the Head of Sales, the bloody file had kept a record of the original name which showed up whenever you hovered the cursor over the file… bollocks.

I can only imagine their disbelief when they saw that and opened it up to find I had failed to include an opening slide announcing my resignation, as it appeared to be perfectly set up for a pretty ballsy exit strategy.

So note to self - if you're going to be bitter, probably best not to mess around with technology. Especially if you're one of the old dickheads who fondly remembers the original Clip Art and has the IT skills to go with it.

Faux pas 9

Discrete entrances

I'm slowly putting more pieces of the puzzle together to figure out why my sales career didn't last longer than the average 15 year old's relationships.

The pivotal sales retreat was a chance to mingle with even more of the team, because surprisingly the attendees weren't just made up of the sales team - they included the folks who were essential to delivering the complete package for customers, such as some of the consultants we employed. This made for great entertainment. Take Eric for example. Eric had the body of a weightlifting 20 year old, face and fashion appearance of a 50 year old, and drinking ability of an immortal. Then there was Angus, the fiery Scotsman who lived off of nothing but Haribo, flapjacks and tequila - the resulting blend of sugar and alcohol in his bloodstream meant it was like dealing with a paranoid schizophrenic, and not only that but one who was strategically using them as his uppers and downers. It should come as no surprise that there was a time when we were at an airport getting ready to jet off to another company sales retreat in Germany, and the heady mix of my inability to refrain from dishing out antagonistic quips and Angus' barely hidden disdain for me resulted in him threatening to punch me in the face for being a "cocky little twat". Harsh but fair, I had to admit. Still, it made for an interesting group dynamic as we were ushered out of the bar and towards our gate's waiting area by colleagues less concerned about the preservation of my face than their ability to reach the mecca of an all-inclusive company retreat in Germany.

Funnily enough, this wasn't the only time I'd found myself dallying outside the behavioural norms at airports. I'm sure 97% of passengers follow the same routine of get bored and impatient at security, march off afterwards to try and find somewhere to eat/drink, sit and talk about upcoming trip over said food and drink, rush to get overpriced snacks/water/reading material from the shops, then stomp to the departure gate only to wait an eternity and get bored and impatient again. Ah yes, the circle of (airport) life. On the trip back from that particular sales retreat in Germany (hmmm, perhaps Germany was the common denominator with my airport issues…) I found myself once again coming undone thanks to my old nemesis - medium-strength lager.

Still transporting a fair amount of alcohol in my veins from the night before (the Germans really know how to throw a party - unlimited beer, bratwurst and fire-breathing ladies dancing above clubbers on podiums. Need I say more?!) I was a mess thanks to our ridiculously early flight home. So much so that I apparently fell asleep standing up in the hotel lobby whilst waiting for our minibus, with my colleagues not realising (or caring, the fuckers) that I was still stood in the lobby as they climbed on-board. I only woke up when the automatic sliding door I was stood near opened to let some guests through into another part of the hotel and it sent me flying into a wall. Not a great time to be a liability, especially after we were catching the minibus with my old friend, the MD.

Eventually getting to the airport we all woke up a bit more and started joking about. It was all light-hearted fun, and we were all in good spirits - even Angus didn't threaten to smash my face in for once. Getting to the security check area I was feeling a little cheeky, but remembering where I was I kept it fairly tame as I didn't want to get into the same world of shit that my old friend Nick ended up. He got in trouble when his lips (and imagination) were loosened by some medication he took which was designed to help him overcome his fear of flying, but instead resulted in him being interrogated for hours on end in JFK airport and stranding his whole family after making a quip about a bomb whilst waiting in the queue for security.

Getting the usual *beep beep beep* off of the metal detectors (I've now assumed there must be a metal pellet lodged somewhere in me from an air rifle mishap when I was younger) I was firmly but politely requested to step to one side for the closer scan with a handheld metal detector. The security guard stepped towards me, his attempt to smile barely covering his boredom and contempt for the job. Deciding he needed to be as chipper as the rest of us and enjoy some light-hearted banter to brighten his day and get him laughing with us, I decided to try and break through his glumness and get him on-side.

Well that was a fucking mistake.

As he asked me to stand up straight and stretch my arms out, I decided to make small talk as he started scanning. But he still didn't bite and give me any response in return, so I went fishing again.

As he started scanning my torso and moving down to my crotch, I chuckled and in my best German accent said "Oh, hello" the camp inflection in my voice undeniably insinuating I was enjoying this a bit too much. Looking at me quizzically for a moment he then raised an eyebrow, smiled and then got down on his knees to perform a ridiculously slow scan up each leg. I mean, if you thought someone was taking the piss and mock-hitting on you, then would you honestly get down on your knees and slowly… ah. It was at that point I then realised maybe I'd been bantering with a gay Germany security guard. Well. I hadn't anticipated that.

Deciding to try some more humour when I really should've just tried to snap us out of the homoerotic fandango we had just embarked on, I tried one last throw of the dice.

"Well at least buy me a drink first before you…"

I was cut off as the guard suddenly went into warp speed, rapidly launching the metal detector up my inside thigh and slamming it firmly into my testicles. The smile was immediately wiped from my face, replaced with a gurning and bulging of every vein in my neck as I struggled to contain the pain coursing through my entire body, which pushed me to the edge of passing out, vomiting, or both.

Deciding I needed to steady myself I leant forward, still groaning, and rested my hands on his shoulders. Well, that really set him off.

"DO NOT TOUCH ME!" he yelled in my face, stepping back and removing the nice little perch I'd been resting momentarily against, nearly causing me to stack it right there and then from the cocktail of pain and alcohol cruising through my body. I kept myself upright but didn't manage to avoid causing a scene and making it look like I was being a proper little sex pest.

So he wasn't gay and just didn't like my tipsy bullshit. Well played *Sicherheitsbeamter*, well played indeed.

Interestingly, that wasn't even my only faux pas with security, airport or otherwise. When I was a teenager we'd been taken on a school trip to the Old Bailey in London to experience first-hand a court case. I think they wanted us to learn about the trial and sentencing aspects of the justice system after we'd read the book and been to the theatre to see the adaptation of An Inspector Calls.

What we in actual fact learned were two very valuable life lessons.

The first was as a result of listening to the court case. I genuinely have no idea why the teachers didn't get us to leave the public gallery once it became clear how fucked up the court case was. Maybe they too were completely transfixed, open mouthed in shock at the details unfolding before us. Maybe they wanted to scare the shit out of us and get us to behave when we returned to the classroom, the fear of ending up like the poor lad in the court case the incentive to not stray too far from the middle-class education path we'd been on up to then.

Either way, I don't think anyone would forget the bat-shit crazy case we heard and the lessons we all took away from it.

Essentially there was a young lad from up North who fell on hard times whilst still really young, which was really sad to hear. It had the classic hallmarks of so many bad childhoods - a stepdad who liked to hit him, no attention or love from the parents and the threat of harm from older kids on the estate. Deciding to get away from it all, he got on a train and headed for the bright lights of London.

Being young, without money and needing help in a city, especially one like London, is generally only going to lead to bad things, and sadly this lad didn't buck that trend. He was befriended by an older guy who took him under his wing and gave him a place to stay, but pretty soon it became clear that to still have a place to stay and food on his plate he'd have to do some favours for other older guys. He essentially pimped him out, and started to get pretty abusive too. Stuck with nowhere else to go, the lad started to rebel.

It started with petty things like drinking the guy's booze and stealing. Then it got pretty dark, when it was revealed he'd stabbed the guy's pet budgie to death with a pencil, before ending the whole thing with a crescendo of darkness as we were told how one morning the lad had found the guy's dressing gown and proceeded to stuff the murdered budgie in one pocket, and unleash the fury of his arse into the other. Bleak. I can only imagine he wanted the guy to put it on and not realise before shoving his hands in his pockets and getting them covered in budgie entrails and steaming hot shit. But it turned out the old chap wasn't suffering from anosmia and so could smell the death and faeces a mile off. Oh well, better luck next time lad, but a solid 10/10 for effort.

I'll never forget the teachers and all of us sucking in the fresh air when we stepped out of The Old Bailey, like we'd been slowly suffocating from all the depravity of London's seedy underbelly.

So there you go, we learned the valuable lesson to not end up as a rent boy in London, stab a budgie to death with a pencil, and leave a combination of dead animals and freshly laid turds in someone's dressing gown pockets, no matter how fucked up they are.

The next lesson was far less intense, but still worth learning.

It was actually from earlier on that day, on our way into the public gallery to watch the court case. It was taking ages to queue up a really long flight of stairs to get to the security desk before we could even enter the courtroom, and so being bored teenagers our conversation immediately turned to the classic topic du jour - girls. Having accidentally stumbled across someone's hidden stash of porn in the local woods as a nine year old, my fascination with the opposite sex had been in full flight for a number of years, yet thanks to the gift of ginger hair, glasses and acne I had been devoid of any interaction with one. Hell, at that point in my life I'd have been elated if one even spoke to me.

As we got closer to the security gate at the top of the stairs we saw the security guard. She was absolutely stunning, and with her air of authority and tight-fitting shirt we were all in love. Allowing my brain to freestyle once again, I turned to my friends.

"Watch this," I said smugly as I stuffed my house keys into my pants.

You see, she was manning a metal detector stand, and I could see her giving people a real good pat-down to find whatever had set off the alarm. It was only natural that my teenage brain put two and two together and came up with seventy.

Losing myself in the anticipation of her having to search really hard to find the keys in my pants, I failed to notice something quite important until the last minute.

Her shift had ended.

And not only that, but she was replaced by an old, stony-faced, and dare I say paedo-esque old man. Fuck.

By this point I was only three people away from the security gate, and I started to panic.

"No, no, no, no…" I muttered, fumbling with the zip on my trousers as I desperately tried to fish the keys out and put them in my coat pocket like a normal person, and avoid a Jimmy Savile rub-down from the boney-fingered guard who was now just a few feet away.

My friends couldn't stop pissing themselves laughing as the queue in front of us cleared and I was left standing there with my hand stuck down my trousers, rummaging away with a frantic look on my face.

The security guard looked at me with contempt. Quite right to be honest - I would've been disapproving of any dirty little herbert I came across having a rummage in a public place. He soon upgraded it to disgust when I pulled my hand out and showed him the keys to avoid any confusion as to what was about to set off the alarm. He knew exactly what I'd been up to. Of course he did - you don't work with a beautiful lady like that and not have guys of all ages being complete and utter pests.

After passing the security checks sans house keys I shuffled into the courtroom, my head hanging in shame and keen avoid a repeat situation, much like the poor Northern lad.

As for the rest of my security faux pas? Well you'll hear all about them in a later chapter.

Anyway, back to the annual sales retreat.

Clocking the likes of Eric and Angus made me pause and have a moment of concern, which quickly morphed into a moment of sinister glee in anticipation of the carnage that lay ahead, for these were the techies. Forget the sales people, the techies were the real wild ones. And so the annual drinkfest began, with management in one section of the country house enjoying fine Italian Barolos and Argentinian Malbecs with their porterhouse steaks, and the rest of us in another section steadily gorging ourselves on filthy burgers and cheap pints.

Rumour has it there was drinking games, nudity and even a stolen golf cart tearing up the immaculate grounds of the venue… Sadly I don't remember much beyond 8pm, and in fact don't remember anything after 10pm until I woke at 9am the next day. I knew mornings and I were about as compatible as a vegan and a fox hunter, and so I'd set three alarms as a failsafe to wake me up in time for breakfast at 7am, all in a bid to make sure I was front and centre for the CEO kicking off the company's plans for the year head at 9am.

9am... shit!

Somehow, against all odds, I'd managed to sleep through all three alarms. On the one hand I was absolutely furious with myself for sleeping in, but on the other hand I was curious as to how loud a noise would have to be to wake me from my drunken slumber (it turns out it's even louder than a fire alarm as I found out a few years later in another debacle).

I like to think I got ready at the kind of breakneck pace that you see in a time-lapse video, but there's every chance I was moving at the pace of a chameleon jacked up on ketamine. Throwing my clothes on, filling my mouth with toothpaste to clean with a finger on the way, I even tried to put my contact lenses in despite the fact I'd slept in them. Yep, I was still wasted. Unnerved in the face of certain lateness I raced down to the conference room.

Needless to say, as I got to the foyer outside the room I could hear the CEO in full swing. Bollocks. Reeking of booze, dishevelled and shuffling along like one of the zombies from The Walking Dead, I decided to try and sneak into the back of the room and slip into the shadows, observing the ramblings from behind the safety of my closed eyes.

Fearing a classic 'squeaky door hinge moment' ruining my discreet entrance, I decided the only way to do it was with controlled speed. I turned the door handle, blinked hard and willed my body to move.

Pushing open the door firmly and stepping into the room I was immediately taken aback by how bright it was at the back of the room. I honestly thought it would be darker. I then stopped dead in my tracks. Oh shit. You have got to be kidding me, I thought. In my hungover state I had gotten the doors to the conference room completely mixed up – I hadn't snuck into the back of the room at all, I had instead burst onto the stage, in full view of the entire company, right next to the CEO...

Deciding that unless I took a dump on the stage there really wasn't anything else I could do to lower my standing in this company, so I ashamedly trudged down the steps, off the stage and found a chair at the back of the room. It was from there where I would hide, trawl the internet for 'world's loudest alarm clocks', and try to remember at least one thing the CEO said so I could pass the informal test we'd get from the MD in the office the next day.

That was just one of many incidents in my life where I knew I wasn't any good at drinking and really should just find another vice, but I didn't like smoking, couldn't afford drugs and wasn't a huge fan of sweets, so wound up chalking off several more absurd drinking-related incidents from the bucket list of shame before I came to my senses and decided to only get truly hammered once or twice a year. I find drinking can either heighten a party or numb the pain. That's why I only drink on my birthday and my wedding anniversary. I'll let you guess which of the benefits of drinking I seek on what occasion!

Faux pas 10

The writing's on the ~~wall~~ turd

It's not just as if I woke up one day and found myself in the habit of saying the wrong thing, doing the wrong thing, or acting the wrong way. No, whilst this is a long-standing habit it definitely has a beginning. If you want to know when my career suicide began, we need to go way back to when I was nine years old to find the earliest examples of me failing at what is effectively the first stage of work - Primary School.

I always loved being the joker. I got a huge sense of delight from making others laugh. I still do. The old 'drawing a cock on someone else's notepad' gag has stood the test of time well. It was like a drug. Well, at that age I didn't really get the concept of drugs, so I'll compare it to the most relevant thing for me at the time – it was like a pack of Skittles, packed to the rafters with E numbers before the fun police came along and took them all out. I just couldn't get enough. On a related note, I actually became so obsessed with sugary snacks as a child that my parents put a child-lock on the cupboard that housed all the sweet treats. I was 10 years old. In a running battle similar to the attempts of inmates to smuggle contraband into prison and the subsequent efforts by guards to intercept it and deny them the pleasure, I managed to figure out how to open each child-lock they deployed until they eventually upped the ante and installed a near adult-proof lock on the cupboard. Undeterred, I quickly managed to overcome the Fort Knox-style security and soon escape with the loot – as a child I was clearly both a joker and a chubby little shit.

But back to being the joker – it was a glorious age where joke shops still thrived, there was no YouTube or satellite TV pushing hundreds of channels of entertainment into kids' tiny yet fertile minds, and no mobile phones. You had to make your own entertainment. And that I did. The jokes and pranks started out small-scale at first: putting a fake fly in someone's water; putting a cracked glass sticker onto one of the windows; pushing the girls I liked into a hedge. You know, the classics. But the boys, they cried out for more, and so determined to be held aloft on their shoulders and have them cheer my name in the playground (I'll admit I had some pretty lofty ambitions to be revered) I took on my greatest mission yet – putting a fake dog turd in the evil Headmistress' office.

Nowadays it seems quite tame, but back then this was like trying to break into Buckingham Palace to steal their finest jewellery. And so in the joke shop one Saturday I studied the three fake turds on sale: the small, curly turd that looked like it had been deposited by a Chihuahua; a mid-range beauty with good girth and a near-perfect curl to it; and then the behemoth, a true beast of a turd that I gasped at in shock and awe. It was like King Kong's finger. No, that beast would have to wait for another day – I decided that the mid-range beauty would be the one. Standing at the counter and handing over my hard-earned pocket money I collected the small bag with the perfect turd in it, turned on my heel and literally skipped out of that wonderful Aladdin's cave of treasures. The plan was afoot.

In addition to confectionery I also had a moderately unhealthy exposure to action movies (Rambo was my idol at age 10, which explains a lot) and a desire to be a ninja, which culminated in me treating Operation Deposit as if it were critical to the future of the world. These delusions would continue until I was well into my thirties, at which point reality would hit hard and in the blink of an eye I'd go from Peter Pan to a married father of two who spends his weekends in soft play, Ikea and Tesco. Adulting is shit - Peter Pan was bang on the fucking money with not wanting to grow up.

The big day eventually arrived. I knew the Headmistress would be in a class covering an absent teacher, which presented me with the perfect window of opportunity. Making my excuses of needing the toilet, I left my class and walked towards them. A quick scan showed nobody was around, and so I darted into a corridor that led to the office. My back against the wall, I slowly edged along until I turned the corner and could see the gates of hell (her door, for those of you not familiar with the underworld that was Mrs Baxter's office). Listening for any sound that could indicate someone was inside, I decided the coast was clear and quickly shuffled up to the door and pushed it open. I was inside. Quickly breathing in the air of power and authority, I decided there was no time to savour the moment and instead looked for the perfect place to deposit the turd. It couldn't be too obvious, nor could it be too discrete. Opting for the corner of her desk I delicately placed it on the carpet, giggled, and left the office, emerging victorious into the darkness of the corridor. To paint the picture of how utterly ridiculous my mind is, I still genuinely to this day see films of spies and special forces soldiers sneaking around buildings and afford myself a smug little grin and think to myself that it's a piece of piss, and after the success of Operation Deposit I could easily do it. Delusions of grandeur I believe my therapist calls them.

Returning to class I sat down with a smile on my face and whispered to my best friend Nathan about the deed. With a look that managed to simultaneously merge horror, glee and excitement in one (incidentally the same emotions my face conveyed when my wife told me I was going to be a parent for the first time), he quickly turned and told one of his friends, and before I knew it a wildfire of Chinese whispers had roared into life and swept through the entire school. I was one step closer to being held aloft by a crowd in the playground as fighter jets flew overhead and fireworks lit up the sky... My delusions were reaching obscene levels, but I loved it.

Later that day, though, I was brought crashing down when the Headmistress hauled me into her office. Still aiming to keep up the pretence of having never set foot in the hallowed ground of her office before, I looked around in amazement as I stepped in, my mouth slightly open for the perfect dramatic effect. My God, I was born for the stage.

But she was having none of it. "I know it was you," she said.

"Hmmm?" I replied, my eyebrows nearly touching the ceiling as I pursed my lips and tilted my head to the side, as if I'd misheard her. This was normally the action one of my parents took after I'd given them some back-chat and they wanted to either double-check what I said or force me to apologise. It took me several bollockings to realise the right answer was just to apologise, and never to repeat what I'd originally said.

"The fake dog poo. I know you put it in my office. Why did you do it?"

"I don't know what you mean," I objected, "I've never been in your office before."

Something wasn't right. She looked so confident. I was starting to get angry – which little shit had snitched on me, whipping my moment of glory away from me before I'd even had the chance to fully appreciate being a hero? I bet it was Nathan, he was a wily little bugger and I bet he'd not forgiven me for launching his favourite Action Man into his Mum and Dad's fire.

"Then did someone else put your prank poo here?" she offered.

"I don't know why you think it's mine, Miss."

"Well, that's because your initials are on the underside of it."

Ah. Yes. Well that was definitely a problem. Operation Deposit was about to fail because I had put my bloody initials on the evidence. Honestly, you cannot get more amateur than that. There's brain dead criminals in jail who tried to rob a corner shop with their finger pointing through their hoodie pocket to mimic a gun who'd smirk at my failings here. But in my defence, I'd spent an awful lot of pocket money on that turd and it was a prized possession, bound to give me years of comedy gold, and so fearing it would be lifted by one of my many light-fingered school friends, I had indeed initialled it.

Thinking on my feet I replied "Well it could be Tamsyn Howley's – she's got the same initials as me!"

"Tamsyn is off sick today, so it can't have been her. Plus, the writing of 'Hands off, this is T.H.'s' matches yours, so I'm afraid we'll need to talk to your parents."

Well, the game was well and truly up - she had me bang to rights and therein began my earliest experience of failing horribly in the workplace. Sadly, whilst the awkwardness has remained the same the repercussions have tended to grow as the years have gone by. Oh to be Peter Pan and never grow up...

Faux pas 11

The lost art of miming

I'd always thought of the art of miming as being a wonderful thing that could help people communicate no matter what the situation. Can't speak the same language? No problem! Just mime. We've all been there, doing the classic 'scribbling on a piece of paper' mime to get a waiter on holiday to fetch the bill. Far easier than learning "L'addition s'il vous plaît." Mind you, we even do it when we know the waiter can speak perfect English – it's that ingrained in our psyche.

Music too loud in a bar to hear what someone's saying? No problem - mime away! I'm confident that at one point in every person's life they've ended up doing the classic tipping an imaginary glass in front of the face routine to signal "Do you want a drink?" to a friend in a nightclub. Whether they nail it or look like they're asking for a blowjob, however, is another question entirely. It's a fine line between glass-tipping and blow-jobbing, which undoubtedly has led to one or two rather awkward encounters in bars where no amount of miming can save them!

So given its ability to transcend language barriers you can understand why the mime was chosen as my tool of choice when on the London Underground I wanted to make a quip to someone who didn't speak English. You will also soon understand why there are some occasions when it's better to simply let the moment pass to avoid being labelled an utter lunatic and pervert.

It was a hot summer's day in London. I was exhausted thanks to a four hour meeting and the fact the Underground has the incredible ability to amplify any temperature - often to the point in summer where even the air movement from a train pulling into a platform feels like your face has been shoved in front of a furnace. It is on days like that when being in London becomes some kind of sick endurance game that even Channel 4 wouldn't commission.

Stepping off the train and heading towards the escalator with the mass of fellow commuters and tourists, I saw a girl who must have only been about 10 years old step away from her Mum and choose to run up the 100+ stairs instead of taking the escalator. What the fuck, I thought to myself - given the stifling heat that was utter madness. But fair play to her, she bounded up those steps without even breaking into a sweat. I'd have been hyperventilating by the fifth one. As I got on the escalator behind the Mum I said "Wow! I wish I had her energy!" She looked at me quizzically, then cocked her head slightly and frowned - the universal sign for 'Eh?'. Thinking she might have been distracted and not really listening to me the first time round I said it again, this time a bit louder (a common tactic I have to employ with my wife, like there's some kind of marital echo). This time she stared at me blankly and responded with something in a language I didn't recognise at all, which frustrated me as I wanted her to chuckle at my really-not-worth-explaining-any-more quip.

Undeterred, I deployed the mime.

Pointing at her young daughter bounding up the stairs, I

then mimed her bounding up them, but as I was stood on an escalator that seemed like it was a staircase to heaven I made the decision to avoid becoming TfL's new accident poster boy, and so rather than running on the spot I kept my feet firmly planted to the steel grate, and instead just swung my arms back and forth with a slight twisting of the hips to mimic her heading up those stairs. Picture a Dad dancing at a wedding and you've got it in one. Coupled with this I was puffing out air to show the physical exertion side of things (I take my miming very seriously), before then pointing to myself and grinning, raising my eyebrows and going "Eh, eh!"

At the time I thought that was a pretty good way to show I was thinking "Wow! I wish I had her energy!" From the look of horror on the Mum's face, and the fact that she ran up the next 25 steps, grabbed her daughter's hand and hurried off to safety, what I'd actually insinuated was that I was a brazen sexual predator who was keen to rut her daughter and exert a great amount of effort in doing so…

Quickly realising this, and not wanting to get arrested at the next turnstile, I tried to proclaim my innocence. It was at this point I should have just hung my head in shame and shuffled off to catch my train home. Instead my brain reverted to type, slammed the gear stick into neutral and let my mouth run away without a second thought, leading me to shout after her "But I'm not a paedophile, honest!" In hindsight this probably also wasn't a great idea considering I was stood in a packed Underground station in the middle of the school holidays.

I was subsequently given the kind of wide berth reserved purely for drunks, the homeless, and of course, perverts, as

I sheepishly made my way to the platform, telling myself this was definitely the last time I would ever try to mime.

Faux pas 12

Mum's the word

Having moved to the engineering firm a few years before this next faux pas, I found I was fine at mingling with the guys who liked to play football and go for beers on a Friday after work, but with the uncanny ability to pick up an injury every week (I once even pulled my hamstring trying to put my football boots on) and having neither a liver nor girlfriend that would cope with me drinking heavily every single Friday, I decided a change was needed. I needed to join something that could give me opportunities to mingle, have fun and not edge closer to developing liver cirrhosis on a weekly basis.

One day I received an email with the answer: the company social club. My girlfriend had suggested I give it a go for some time, but much like her suggestion to not greet her with the helicopter when emerging from the shower each morning, I had firmly ignored it.

A heady mix of bowling, cricket, theatre and curries, it was the perfect opportunity for me to build some new friendships within the business, and see what life was like for the unadventurous middle-aged office worker. My first foray into this new world was the annual meeting to discuss the calendar of activities for the coming year. Stepping into the small and over-crowded room, I was surprised to see a whole range of people: from the young hipsters of the business development team to the sarcastic techies from IT, and even the decrepit pensioners of the policy team. It appeared the social club was actually pretty diverse.

Spotting a few people I knew, I sidled up next to them and settled in for what I expected to be an hour of my life that I would never get back.

Surprisingly, it was a very light-hearted affair, with quite a lot of banter and everyone clearly feeling relaxed. By the end it felt like we were down the pub, which was brilliant because unlike going to the pub I wouldn't wake up in debt, on the sofa and with remnants of the ubiquitous late-night takeaway smeared across both me and said sofa.

As the meeting wrapped up and we were all filtering out, one of the guys piped up "Hey, how come you didn't make it to the meeting this morning? Only interested when it's an easy one, huh?" Checking to see who he was levelling that accusation at, and then realising it was me, I stopped as he continued "What were you so busy doing that you couldn't make it?" A few of the guys stopped walking and turned and looked. The stage had been set, the challenge of a cutting response thrown down squarely at my feet, and they waited with bated breath ready for me to respond with something witty. But shit – what the hell would I say? Normally, giving banter was easy because I didn't think, I slipped my brain into neutral and let my mouth run away with it. But I was enjoying the job and was determined to not fuck it up so I'd put the brakes on my potty mouth. But wait - technically it was the social club, I thought. For a moment I had an outer body experience, and after realising I was worrying about a bloody social club I started to contemplate what had happened to my life… Should I just go to the pub again and forget this foray into grown-up socialising? Or should I actually grow up and just be sensible? Then I realised I'd been thinking all of that whilst they just stood there and watched me. Panicking, and realising I needed to respond with something, anything, just to reassure them I wasn't having a stroke, I regressed to my teenage self, which is never, ever, a good thing, and snapped back "Why don't you ask Ed's Mum?!"

Brilliant, I thought, laughing as I turned to stroll victorious through the gauntlet of the guys watching this little exchange. I was poised, ready to claim the spoils of victory. Except nobody else laughed. There was silence. And not just any old silence. Oh no, it was a strained, tense, so-awkward-people-actually-grimaced kind of silence.

Realising I'd completely misjudged the boundaries of this social club lot, I scurried down the corridor to the safety of my team's office, wondering if I could find a way of figuring out where those boundaries were. I mean, if they got offended by a Mum joke, all hell would definitely break loose the minute I called someone a cunt in a friendly game of badminton.

Later that day I remembered my girlfriend knew Ed and some of the guys who seemingly had a far too mature sense of humour for my joke to land, so I decided to try some sleuthing to figure out what on earth happened. I mean, I'm no Michael McIntyre but equally I shouldn't be dying on my arse when throwing out middle-class barbs and Mum jokes.

"Hey, I went to that social club meeting earlier like you suggested."

"Oh that's great hun, how did it go?"

"It was alright actually, until on the way out when one of

Ed's mates tried to give me grief over missing an earlier meeting – he basically called me out in front of the other guys for being lazy."

"Oh no, really? That's a bit cheeky."

"Well don't worry, it wasn't a problem because I managed to think on my feet – it wasn't my best work, but I managed to save myself…just."

"Well done hun."

"Yeah but they're all a bunch of middle-aged prudes through aren't they? I mean not one of them laughed at my quip back at him, the miserable bastards."

"Oh that's a shame, normally they're game for a laugh."

"Well clearly they're above Mum jokes."

"What?"

That got her attention.

"Mum jokes – he asked what I was doing earlier as I was clearly too busy to make a meeting, so I said 'Ask Ed's Mum.' Who doesn't love a Mum joke?!"

Her face was stony, "Tom – you dick, Ed's Mum died last year…"

Ahhh. Shit.

Yep, I'd been a massive arsehole.

It was at this point I too went silent, grimaced and pulled the kind of face you'd pull if you saw a really bad car crash, or your parents having sex. They're both monstrous images that will leave you damaged for life. And so with that, I learned lesson #73 in the banter manual of life – Thou Shalt Never Bring Parents Into Jokes With New People.

Surprisingly Ed never held it against me, although come to think of it I now have my doubts about the social club night out where he 'slipped' and the contents of his pint soon made itself at home on my trousers...

Faux pas 13

Shortcuts in IT = shortcuts to P45

I am so grateful for advances in technology. There's the big ones like the ability to detect and treat cancer, or taking the size of a computer from something that would fill your average living room down to something that fits inside a watch. But I also love the little advances that make life easier, quicker and more efficient - like search engines remembering what you often hunt for, or autocorrect. But sometimes with great power comes responsibility. And when that responsibility is handed over to us mere mortals, it ends up as 'with great power comes great risk of ending up in the shit'. Doesn't quite roll off the tongue as well, but I think it's a bit closer to reality for most of us.

A key part of my role at the engineering firm was to liaise with a Government department on all kinds of mind-numbing things like project finances, project progress reports, risk reports, equipment installation updates… you get the idea. Like I said, mind-numbing. But these clever folk down in London were classic civil servants and loved a boring report to read whilst sat in their boring offices drinking their boring drinks and counting down the days until their not-so-boring pension could be collected. As you can tell, I'm not a fan. I don't think many people are. But I soon came to respect, be grateful for, and even like one of them!

We'd been delivering a multi-million Pound project using some Government money for a few years and it's fair to say they'd caused us a fair bit of grief to get the funding to simply get it started, and beaten us half to death with a contract that would make a treaty between Russian and Ukraine seem like a mere gentleman's agreement. Tensions between the civil servants and our team were at an all-time low, and whilst we'd been keen to not just lie down and take it in the regular 'meetings' (aka verbal and psychological beatings) our Legal team advised us against this. Something about not biting the hand that feeds you.

Keen to keep tabs on us, the Government team would seek email updates in addition to the meetings, and we had a key contact to email as well as a team inbox so they could all chuckle at our fraught efforts to meet their ever-maddening demands. Having learned about what kind of employee I was, specifically my ability to go into corporate zombie mode at any moment, our Legal team was keen for me not to derail years of hard work and potential funding in the future, so I was told in no uncertain terms after my first email to the key contact and the group inbox to never email them again. Legal would be the only point of contact from our company regarding this particular project moving forward.

How dare they, I immediately thought when I was told of Legal's command. How sensible, I then thought straight after! Prevention is definitely better than cure, and they'd clearly seen an idiot on the loose before and knew how to wrap me up and keep me away from anyone with any influence.

Accepting my email ban, I happily carried on working on the project and feeding key results into the people who were trusted enough to hit 'Send' on the email. It had been a busy old week when this next faux pas came about and I was bored and needing to escape, so when the weekend came that's what I did. Essentially I went out and rediscovered my love of red wine in a local bar, stumbling home barely able to remember my own name, and spent the next day recovering on the sofa watching movies that my struggling brain could cope with. I really loved that form of escapism. And looking back now that I've got kids, I yearn for even a snippet of that life again – my only hopes of escaping the madness and constant demands for my time are the five blissful hours of sleep at night and five minutes in the toilet in the morning, four of which are spent trawling through messages on my phone.

Monday morning came all too soon. Monday mornings were still not my friend. They were more like a noisy neighbour when neither of you are renting – you know it's inevitable that there's going to be frustration, but there's nothing really you can do to avoid it for quite some time. But it still doesn't stop you getting livid and considering doing something wild with potentially devastating consequences to stop the frustration. Although I'd like to reassure my lovely neighbour June that even though you watch the Antiques Roadshow loud enough for it to register on the richter scale I won't be coming round with a baseball bat to sort it out. Not yet anyway.

Mark was a good friend in our team, and we often exchanged stories about our weekends on a Monday morning. On this particular Monday it was no different, although he was 'working from home' so we all know what that means – wake up at 10am, watch Bargain Hunt until 11am, send an email, watch some more TV until lunch, maybe have an afternoon nap, send another email, maybe watch Homes Under The Hammer, a bit of porn, then do one final email before it's time to call it a day. As a result we'd have to swap our tales of escapism and mild alcoholism via email.

I'd still not heard from him by lunch, so I decided to send the first email. Now obviously I wasn't a complete muppet and knew to avoid using all the main expletives and even a few random ones that a friend in IT told me they scanned outgoing emails for to flag them up to HR, but it was nothing a good old asterisk here or there couldn't help slip under the radar – it meant I didn't really have to give a sh*t about what I wrote or who I called a tw*t. It went as follows:

'Hey buddy, how was the weekend?

Did you get on it?! Did you see Julia again? Bet you've got plenty of reasons to be smiling this morning ;-)

I had such a sh*t week dealing with all that b*llocks on that massive project that I needed to get out of this place and get piss*d! I was pretty toasted by about 8pm on Friday and then properly went out with Rob and got on the Jagerbombs... I was absolutely sh*tfaced! :-P

Spent the rest of the weekend watching old school movies – think I watched about three Jurassic Park movies on Saturday... was awesome! Nothing like sitting in your pants watching TV whilst stuffing your face with sugar and eating all kinds of random sh*t! Living the dream! :-D

Tom'

Pretty standard non-contentious stuff, and if for any

reason it was picked up by IT and handed over to those totalitarians in HR, I was confident it would just be a slap on the wrists and an informal warning. I quickly started typing his name, hit the tab button on my keyboard to autofill the rest of his name (he's got more letters in his name than a village in rural Wales) and clicked 'Send'. Cracking on with my day, I kept checking to see if Mark had finally emerged from his daytime TV binge into the land of the living, but there was nothing. Useless bastard. Then all of a sudden I got the pop up to say I had a new email, and I could tell from a quick glance at the subject that it was a reply to my email (we didn't tend to get many emails with the title "Beers and dinosaurs!"). Quickly opening up my inbox I double clicked the email to read it, frowning slightly as I did so as I started to realise something wasn't quite right.

Oh shit. Something really wasn't right at all. This was a reply to my email alright, but it sure as hell wasn't from Mark... And then I saw it. The reply was from our key contact at the Government using the group email account... You know when you stub your toe and you grit your teeth, sharply suck in the air, close your eyes, tense up and raise your head to the sky? That is exactly what I did in that moment, before saying "fucking hell!" loud enough to make most people within about 30 feet of me look up from their laptops and wonder what had happened, curious as there was nothing within about 10 feet of me to stub my toe on.

It's one thing to get called out by HR on sending personal emails with a few (albeit asterisked-out) expletives, but to send one to an entire Government department, and one that has the ability to deny you funding to continue operating in that field, well that was potentially career-ending. For both me and my team... Yep, I'd say that was my biggest cockup to date, and one in which the odds of finding a P45 on my desk by the end of the week had been slashed so much that I was already thinking what I was going to put on my soon-to-be-drafted CV to cover up this travesty.

As my eyes started to flick through the reply, I began wondering how the hell did it happen? What did I do to get it so horribly wrong?! And then I realised – it was the bloody shortcut that had shafted me. You see, it turns out the Government department group email account starts with the same first few letters as Mark's surname, and where I'd gotten lazy and hit the tab key to auto-populate the rest of his email address, for some obscure reason it had instead auto-populated the group email address of this Government department...

IT, often the cause of so much angst and frustration in the workplace, had done it again, but this time it had really upped its game. Well played IT, well played.

Growing up, my parents had taught me a valuable lesson – as my Mum would put it, "Treat others how you would want to be treated," whereas my Dad's take on it was "Make friends with everyone as you might need a favour from them in the future." Sage advice Dad, sage advice indeed – because as my brain finally started to process what I was reading in the response from the Government, it became clear that the key contact had been the first person to spot my ridiculous email, realised I was being a complete muppet by sending it to them, and deleted the email to avoid anyone else seeing it.

What. A. Legend.

It turns out that by spending a few minutes at the end of each meeting talking to him like a human being, rather than a civil servant robot like other companies did, I'd done enough for us to have the smallest of bonds and so compel him to save me from that embarrassment and potential sacking. I will be forever grateful to him. I will also never use the auto-populate shortcut with such careless abandon again!

Faux pas 14

Spell check is not a safety net

I think it's clear for all to see that communication is not my strong point. But having said that, I am surprisingly good at writing reports. I think it's the fact that my mouth can't run away with me, giving my brain a chance to sense check the ramblings of a madman that end up on the page. When I'm really in the flow of bashing out page after page of text, I just wait for the sea of red underlines from the spell checker to fill the page before going through each one quickly and checking the suggested changes before cracking back on.

Whilst it's bang on the money 99% of the time on my computer, sometimes the spell checker on my phone is absolutely ridiculous – how the hell can it suggest 'cunt' when I've typed 'font' but was actually meaning to spell 'don't'? How often must I type 'cunt' for my phone to think that's the word I'm definitely trying to text?! I always think it must be so hard for people with dyslexia or just really poor spelling to rely on spell check for that very reason – when it comes up with about four or five suggestions for the word they've tried to put in, how the hell do they know which one is the right one? I remember a kid in school once asked the teacher how to spell a certain word, but instead of helping him the teacher threw a dictionary at him and told him to look it up himself, before giving the poor lad a detention when he complained he didn't even know where to begin!

Take my friend James – he can't spell for love nor money

(which is probably why both evaded him until the ripe old age of 36) and whether he's texting, WhatsApping or emailing, it takes the powers of deduction of a WW2 code breaker to figure out what the hell he's on about. Take the poor bugger trying to email his wife about the state of his hotel room whilst away on business – whilst trying to spell 'duvet' he ended typing 'doovey'. Using spell check he was faced with the tough choice of 'dove', 'dovely', 'dopey' or 'covey'. He didn't stand a chance. And when you throw autocorrect whilst texting into the mix, all hell can really break loose – not just for James, but for all of us. Take the time when I was using the screen mirroring function to display my phone screen on the TV in our lounge, and show my parents some of our holiday pics from a recent jaunt to Spain. I did this because otherwise due to their ripe old age we have to endure hours of faffing around as they try to find the optimum distance to hold the phone out in front of them to focus on each image, at which point the phone is normally so far away they can't even tell what they're looking at or it's locked due to inactivity.

Whilst going through the holiday pictures and getting the obligatory oooh's and aaaah's from my parents, my brother text me.

"Oooh, what did Daniel say?" my Mum asked.

"Let's take a look," I replied as I showed off the fact they could also see that on screen too. After everyone had seen the message, I offered to type a reply to let him know that they were at our house and we were looking through our holiday snaps. The only trouble is, the autocorrect on my phone decided to reveal my deepest darkest secrets to my parents and wife in crisp HD, all 50" inches of it...

As I started typing out 'Hey Dan, all good down here, Mum and Dad are just flicking through our Spain photos' all was going well until autocorrect waded in and decided to change 'flicking' to 'fingering'. My eyes widened and I quickly deleted it and carefully typed out 'flicking' and moved on to typing the rest of the message in the hope that nobody saw what happened. Bloody technology. Attempting to type 'You're a real legend for helping look after the dog this weekend' got about three words in before it became apparent that autocorrect was lifting its suggestions from my recent searches on porn websites – there's no other way it would change the harmless 'legend' to the parent-cringing 'lesbians'. Shit. There was no way this one went unnoticed – my parents were a little shocked, taking in the fact their grown son was still acting like a schoolboy and searching for filth on the internet, whilst my wife was quietly seething. Once again, the game was up, my phone exposing my sly perusing of all kinds of debauchery and throwing me well and truly under the bus.

"We'll talk about this later," my wife whispered to me. Damn it, I thought, fearing the Spanish inquisition I'd no doubt get over this once my folks had gone home. It was clearly time to wrap it up sharpish and get back to the bloody photos.

The fear was real. I was genuinely terrified of what might pop up on screen next. I should have just disconnected the screen mirroring. I should have done anything other than carry on typing and trying to get the message done as quickly as possible. The air was thick with tension. Everyone's eyes were on the screen. As each word was typed out I could see my family wondering what was going to be revealed about my late-night perusing habits next. With every word that was successfully written without the autocorrect wading in I had a little jolt of panic and immediate relief, making my eyebrows rise higher and higher, like watching someone on You've Been Framed jump from rock to rock when crossing a river – you know something bad could potentially happen at any minute, and the surprise as they get further along without falling in simply builds the tension and excitement even further as they get close to doing it. But they never do. They always slip and fall in. Yet I was adamant I could be the one, I could do this without falling into the pit of shame and awkwardness.

I'd managed a whole sentence without any drama.

Shattering my concentration my Mum piped up, "Can you just ask him to put dinner in the oven at six o'clock? That would be fantastic, thanks love."

"Sure thing," I shot back as I tried to negotiate this final sentence, all that stood between me and safety. Sweet, sweet safety.

'And if you can put the dinner in the oven', I typed, seeing the light at the end of the tunnel, 'that would be gangbang.'

Shit!

"Tom!" my Mum cried out.

"AHHHH!" I wailed, as my hands flew open in shock and I looked wild-eyed at the phone as it dropped to the floor, as if it had just morphed into a giant steaming turd in my hands.

"Are you kidding me?!" my wife snapped at me.

Safety was now a foreign concept, and I was now firmly at the bottom of the pit of shame and awkwardness.

"Shit! I meant to type 'fantastic'!" I said to my wife, my eyes pleading with her to have pity on me.

There was no pity to be had. She was very much deciding how much to tear a strip off of me in front of my parents, and how long the impending sex ban would be. And in that instant she tapped into the natural ability all wives seem to have when arguing with their other halves, managing to process the situation in lightning-fast time and make a deduction that Sherlock would be proud of, before delivering the knock-out blow of a simple yet effective observation.

"So you mean to say you type 'gangbang' more than you type 'fantastic'?"

Hmmm. Fair point. Damn it – she had me dead to rights, I was not getting out of this one.

"Erm, talk about it later?" I suggested, squirming, wincing and letting my voice go so high at the end as I pleaded with her that I sounded like a teenager yet to hit puberty.

Yep, that was definitely the nail in the coffin, and signalled not only the end of me trying to use screen mirroring to show anyone absolutely anything on my phone, but also the end of me seeing a naked lady for quite some time, whether real or digital…

Which brings us full circle back to the situation of spell check not saving me in the corporate world. As I said earlier, I don't check as I type, I just speed through the spell checking corrections for everything when I'm finished. For this particular report I'd been asked to prepare, there were lots of evaluations to write up and explain to the bosses why we should or shouldn't go ahead with particular initiatives. Riveting stuff. A few hours later I was relieved to still be alive after the monotony of talking about analysis, forecasting and investment decisions. How anyone can do that full time I don't know. And I used to work in a lab where I literally had to watch paint dry! My phone rang – it was the boss.

"Are you nearly done with that report yet? I'm keen to get it before the end of the day."

"Yep, nearly finished, I'll get it over to you by 4:30pm."

Balls – it was going to be nigh on impossible to finish it by then, but with a little extra energy, Red Bull and dance music blasting in my ears, I was confident I could find the extra bit of enthusiasm needed to get it across the line. I set to work, typing so quickly as I raced through the remaining sections that it sounded like a troupe of tap-dancing mice were giving the performance of their lives on my desk. It had reached 4:28 and I was very nearly done – result! Just the spell checks to blast through and I'd be there.

Whizzing through the checks and correcting my horrendous and at times near-dyslexic-spelling, I saved the file, attached it to an email and sent it on its way to my boss. I was pretty pleased with myself at managing to get it done in time, and looked forward to wrapping up for the day and awaiting the praise that I was confident would come once he'd read it.

The next day I came in and sure enough found an email from him with his thoughts on the report. As expected, he was full of praise. Leaning back in my chair I relaxed as I read the rest of his points and prepared to make the final tweaks to get it ready for passing on up the management chain. And then I saw his last point.

'You need to pay attention when writing reports as clearly some errors aren't picked up by spell check.'

Balls. My technique of whizzing through the spelling errors at the end clearly wasn't up to scratch. But what could it be? Rather annoyingly he'd not given me any indication of what it was he was referring to. Yeah, thanks Phil, really appreciate that – now I'd have to read through the whole bloody thing to find what he meant. He was clearly keen on teaching me a lesson. And so began the effort of reading through the dullest 13 pages of text I'd ever produced to find the needle in the haystack. Sometimes I loved my job. This was definitely not one of those times.

Even though it was only 13 pages it took forever. I'll be honest I was thinking I'd gotten so bored and switched off halfway through that I must have missed it. But then I spotted it. It literally leapt out at me. How the hell had I not spotted it?! Because there was no bloody red squiggly line underneath, that's why... My failsafe had failed. And he was right – sure as shit, if I'd have just skimmed back through before sending it to him, I'd have spotted it clear as day. There are some words that just jump out. Especially the ones that tend to refer to sex acts. For you see, in the section that was all about the evaluation of something we'd tested, I'd written the following: 'To determine the viability of the solution we carried out thorough anal on the cabinet'. For fuck's sake! Then I remembered – I'd been starting to write that section when he'd called me, and I must have got so distracted when typing out 'analysis' that I stopped part-way through and then carried on unaware once I'd decided to put in place my caffeine and music plan.

And so that was yet another valuable career lesson – never, ever, think that spell check is a 100% safety net, because it is fundamentally flawed for situations where you end up typing utter filth. Perfectly spelt, yes, but filth nonetheless.

If you think my experience is cringeworthy, spare a thought for my poor colleague Alan. Alan is a lovely man, nearing retirement after a solid career, with never a bad word to say about anyone. We all love him because he's always smiling, and always dressed with a shirt, tie and jumper combo, no matter the weather or the day of the week – although on dress-down Fridays he would occasionally rock up sans jumper – he was that wild.

He was also a man of detail and every word spoken, let alone written, was carefully thought through and selected, allowing him to cut through a conversation like a knife through butter with his views. He was very different to a lot of us younger guys, and it was at times like talking to a combination of Gandalf and Alan Sugar, and we respected what he had to say as he was often right.

Eventually I think he started to get a bit annoyed with all the banter, bullshit and general dicking around coming from the younger members of the team, and so one day suggested we create a kind of swear jar by having a tally of each person's potty mouth outbursts up on the office whiteboard. The forfeit was a round of drinks, which for our team could end up being a sizeable amount. I was not exactly thrilled with this idea, because as the son of a soldier and grandson of a sailor I thrived on using edgy, blue and at times downright disgustingly-lewd language throughout my day. Giving it up would be like giving up carbs – I'd baulk at the idea, before promptly telling you to fuck right off. In a previous company where a swear jar was put in place, I ended up racking up a debt of £15 compared to all my colleagues' combined bill of £2.70. Did I mention that was only after two weeks? Until you've been chastised by your wife in the buggy section of a busy Mothercare for grunting "Come on, you fucking cunt!" in anger whilst trying to figure out how the hell you unfurl a Silver Cross pushchair, your swearing isn't an issue. Mine very much is. Nevertheless, I saw it as a chance to turn over a new leaf, and really give it a go.

After several weeks Alan was loving it, chuckling away as he'd overhear an infringement and stride up to the board to chalk it up. There was no escaping his bat-like hearing. We'd agreed after about a month that we should look to wrap it up, tot up the tally for each of us and declare the foul-mouthed winner, aka whose bank balance would be taking the hit down the pub at the next team outing. Once again, I was 'winning', but this time not by much.

Then came the email. Oh yes, the email. It was from Alan.

It was to all the members of a project-specific team, and he had clearly bashed out a hurried reply to an email from one of them seeking a prompt response, because in his haste he'd quite clearly ignored the option to use the spell checker. He evidently had faith in his typing ability. But boy was it misplaced faith... You see, one part of Alan's email went a little like this:

'For the latest monitoring devices, we have made significant progress in deployment – the last cunt revealed a total of 330 installs to January. This is without including the latest batch of devices that have been issued. By my cunt we can expect to see this number reach 380 by April.'

Oh Alan, how we love you. The most mild-mannered man I've ever met had just unwittingly fired off an email full of c-bombs, copying in over a dozen colleagues, direct reports and even some senior management. He was none the wiser. You could tell the minute the email landed in people's inboxes – the bursts of laughter and gasps of shock as people exclaimed "Alan!" gave it away. Poor Alan had no idea, because once again spellcheck had lulled him into a false sense of security, before cruelly whipping the carpet from beneath him and leaving him in an embarrassed heap for all to see. We took it easy on him, after all he's such a nice guy, but we did all delight in going up to the board and chalking up his two strikes, albeit with a multiplier of 10 because they were c-bombs, to leave Alan as the leader of the swear jar challenge and immortalised as the foulest-mouthed engineer of our department. He did protest his innocence, but we were having none of it, and to this day we always joke to new starters or external contacts not to mess with Alan or else they would feel his wrath via an expletive-ridden email. I'm sure he'd prefer to leave a different legacy, but much like nicknames, you get what you're given!

Faux pas 15

C U Next Tuesday? No you won't, you're fired

Dropping the c-bomb is a pretty delicate affair. I guess much like dropping an actual bomb, the effects can be devastating and you need to properly think through its use, the fallout and the risk of collateral damage. Sadly with my mind in the pilot seat and my mouth acting as the doors of the bomber, ready to open at any point, it is far too easy to become an office dictator and start dropping these bombs like our office is a war ground.

It was back during my time temping after university that I got caught out by my free and easy blitzing of office etiquette. I was young, brash and more than a little careless, and I was given a temporary job where I had to call up construction companies and try to sell some kind of product that would bore the tits off even the most nerdy of construction workers. Now when you think about it, how many nerdy construction folk can you think of? Exactly. But before I get lynched by the next mob of scaffolders I walk past, what I'm trying to say is that whilst there's a lot of smart guys in construction, there's a reason why you don't see Barry from Bricklayers R Us on Mastermind rattling off answers on the different chemical compositions of cement - they're focused on practical stuff that actually makes a difference and needs careful consideration.

I wasn't thrilled at the prospect of trying to find this rare nerdy breed of builder, but with the alternative being a salesperson for a prostate-tickling sex toy, I happily agreed.

I shit you not about the sex toy job – and they were expecting me to do pre-sales demonstrations… I dread to think what that would have involved, but one thing was for sure – I wasn't prepared to tickle my prostate or any other man's prostate for a few hundred quid a week, or even a few thousand for that matter, so it was at that point I decided to pull out. Terrible choice of words I know. The innuendos literally come thick and fast with that anecdote – see, it never ends!

Surprisingly it turned out I wasn't too bad at the construction sales job. I managed to strike up a rapport with the guys I called up by using my charm, wit and liberally throwing around phrases I'd remembered from watching programmes like Changing Rooms and Groundforce years ago, praying that I was using them in the right context. I'm pretty sure I only got it right about 50% of the time. The other 50% tended to go a little bit like this:

Me: "So it's pretty wet out there today, ain't it?" (did I mention I also turned into a right geezer as part of my rapport-building act?)

Builder: "Yeah, absolutely pissing it down – I ain't happy."

Me: "I reckon you'll need to screw in the damp proof membrane pretty quick and dot and dab the windows before it gets much worse."

Builder: "Eh? What? Where are you from again? Sod this."

At that point the builder would hang up.

To complicate matters though, I was the only guy on the phones - everyone else was female. This brought its own challenges. Now as a guy in his early twenties, when I was hired and told it was an office full of women my mind jumped straight to thoughts of tanned girls in miniskirts acting all sultry whilst on the phone. Clearly my mind was drifting into the world of soft porn, and of course the reality was as about far from that as you could get - the majority were of an age where the biggest topic of discussion on their fag breaks was how they were coping with the menopause and what happened on Coronation Street last night, with the odd side chat of how to treat varicose veins.

Fuck my life. What nightmare had I become embroiled in?!

The only girl around my age was neither tanned nor a fan of miniskirts. She was, however, quite flirty. This could work, I thought. Weighing up the risks of hooking up with someone in the workplace, I was about to suggest we go for a meal and enjoy a bottle of wine whilst talking about travelling, when she suggested we go to The Eagle, get a few pints of Stella and play the fruit machine. Stella? In The Eagle? Let me just paint that picture for you – this was the roughest pub in town, famed for being the place where the hardest men would drink and then fight with knives, while the women were renowned for being just as aggressive as the men! And there I was: a waif at 10 stone, 5'10" tall (5'11" with my brogues on), a face unable to grow a beard and a penchant for a glass of rosé wine. I think we can all agree that I wouldn't stand a chance of surviving that night. Feeling under pressure and equally knowing the risks of rejecting someone in the workplace, I chirpily agreed, secretly hoping we'd never actually get around to organising a date in The bloody Eagle… At least not until I'd had time to put on a bit of muscle, grow a beard and be able to handle drinking more than one mouthful of Stella without falling over. I wondered if she'd hold on for the 15 years needed for me to achieve that?

After a while it was clear that things weren't exactly going well – the ladies were a close-knit gang, and the fact I didn't smoke, watch Coronation Street or have hot flushes meant I was always destined to be an outsider. Coupled with my give-a-shit attitude and habit of rocking up late (cycling to the office was a real mistake) let's just say they were less than enamoured with me after only a few weeks.

Oddly though, when I fell asleep one day in the lunch room following a heavy night on the rosé (hey, don't judge) they immediately went into mothering-mode and started cooing over me. As I started to come round I could hear them talking, so kept my eyes closed to find out what they were saying.

"Awww, isn't he lovely, look at him."

"He's such a sweetie, isn't he?"

"He is so adorable, he reminds me of my son."

"Mmmm, I wish he was in my bed…"

What the fuck?! It was Stella girl. She was certainly keen, but I was paralysed with fear that I was about to be picked up and carried off to her flat, slung over her shoulder like she was King Kong. I decided it was time to open my eyes and get back to work.

Later that day we were all busy once again harassing builders around the country, rattling off more calls than one of those unrelenting insurance-claim bastards when I spoke to Keith in Leeds. Yeah, I still remember you Keith, you massive twat.

Keith was clearly a wise old tradesman, and knew straight away that I was trying to sell him something. He was grizzly, busy and clearly in no mood for some twenty-something who was fresh out of university to start firing off phrases from TV programmes without a clue what they meant, just to fund his ever-growing love of rosé.

"Yeah, two secs mate," he chimed in part way through my opening spiel, before clearly putting his phone down and carrying on doing what he was doing. Fair enough, I thought, this guy might be delicately balancing up on a roof, or carefully putting the finishing touches on a decorative piece of brickwork. Three minutes went by. Still no word from Keith. In the background I could hear lots of clattering, banging, scraping and talking. Another five minutes went by. Still nothing. I decided to turn up the volume to see if I could hear what was going on and figure out if the reason Keith wasn't talking to me was because he was injured and desperately trying to signal for help, or maybe even stuck and unable to reach the phone. I could save him, I thought. It was then at that point I could hear Keith talking to someone else.

"Yeah I've got this little dickhead on the phone trying to sell me some shit, so I'm just leaving him hanging – bet the silly sod won't hang up!"

What. The. Absolute. Fuck. Not cool, Keith. But I wouldn't back down. I (foolishly) thought that if I held out until he eventually picked up the phone I could somehow convince him that I was determined, had a great product for him, and worthy of five minutes of his time. Deep down I knew this was of course complete bollocks, but I had to try – he had got my back up, and I really needed a bonus.

Ten minutes went by. Eventually, a full thirteen minutes and three games of Solitaire later, he picked up his phone.

"Hi, Keith, it's still Tom here!" I said cheerfully.

"Oh wow, you're still there? Right. Ha! Well, okay mate, what did you want to talk about?"

Yes! Result! I'm in, I thought.

"Well, we've got this fantastic -" BEEEEEEEEEP.

Eh? What was that? I thought. It took a second for my mind to register what the noise was. No, it couldn't be. Surely not. He had. Keith the knobhead builder had led me on - letting me get my hopes up and start my spiel again before hanging up. Holy shit, I was so angry I just couldn't hold it in any more.

"You absolute CUNT!" I shouted down the phone to no one, unable to control my rage. And with that I immediately felt the anger lift from my shoulders, as if it was tied to the word and floated away into thin air. Honestly, it can be quite therapeutic sometimes to drop a c-bomb – why not give it a go next time you're feeling stressed? Although I highly recommend avoiding doing it in Mothercare when the stress of trying to figure out how to unfurl a buggy gets too much… I got an awful lot of glares from the other expectant parents before my wife ushered me out of the store.

Unfortunately, what also floated away was my last chance of staying employed - it turns out that when you're in call centre and penned in like battery-caged chickens, the people either side of you can quite clearly hear what you're saying when you're talking normally, and sometimes the people they're talking to can also hear what you're saying. Apparently when you talk any louder than that, a lot more people can hear you, and evidently when you shout something, the whole room and their customers can hear you – as evidenced by the stunned silence that swept through that room quicker than coronavirus.

I can only imagine how many potential deals the company lost that afternoon, but from the swiftness with which I was booted out, I expect it was a fair few.

Unable to accept the blame, I instead turned my frustration to Keith, and actually spent the next two weeks of my unemployment trying to find Keith in Leeds so I could vent my fury, seek revenge and send him a parcel full of dog shit. Thankfully I had no such luck finding him. It's probably for the best - I wouldn't like to think a) how disgusting it would have been to have created the monstrosity (not least of all because I didn't have a dog so I'd have had to trawl the local parks for dog shit), b) how horrendous it would have been for the poor Royal Mail worker who'd have had to deliver it, and c) what would have happened to me when the Police would no doubt have traced the shitty creation back to the dishevelled pit of unemployment I called my home.

Faux pas 16

The magnets

Roughly 4,000 years ago, a shepherd named Magnes was apparently tending his sheep in a part of northern Greece. He took a step and suddenly found that the nails that held his shoe together and the metal tip of his staff had stuck to the rock he was standing on. Intrigued, he began digging and discovered a material that went on to be known as magnetite - and so began mankind's foray into the incredible world of magnets.

Since then, civilisation has created some fantastic innovations using magnets - from powering speakers in stereos and TVs, to storing data in computers and even providing doctors with invaluable data via MRI scans. It is truly humbling to know that humanity is capable of these feats of creativity, coming up with uses that massively benefit society for years to come.

My incident has none of those traits. It instead makes you realise the stupidity that humanity is capable of, and that Darwin's theory of natural selection (weeding out those unsuitable for carrying forward a species' gene pool) extends to homo sapiens just as much as it does to the rest of the animal kingdom.

During my first year at university I'd torn through my student loan at an alarming rate (surprising how fast thousands of Pounds evaporate when you're drinking 10-15 pints a day), and one day found myself with literally no money - I couldn't even afford a can of Coke. As I searched down the back of the sofa cushions for any spare change (which in a student house lived in by four filthy boys was pretty daunting) to buy something, anything, to eat, I realised I needed a new source of income.

Settling down on the grubby sofa I started wracking my brain, trying to come up with ways in which I could earn some money. Selling drugs? Nope – I wasn't edgy enough. Trafficking drugs? Hell no – if the prostate-tickling job was out the window, this sure as shit was too. Selling my body? Hmmm, worth a bit more thought, until I realised I had such little success offering my body to women for free that there was no way they would happily hand over their hard-earned cash for fifteen minutes of fumbling. Selling crap on ebay? Nah, the post office was miles away, and I didn't have much stuff to sell so would have to resort to nicking things, which I also wasn't overly keen on. Either way, the next option – selling stolen goods? Nope, I'd seen a guy in the pub trying to sell a DVD player and the dopey twat hadn't even stolen the power cable – my OCD wouldn't allow myself to sell on something missing its essential parts, so that idea tanked as well.

Hell, I even considered selling underwear online, but not just any old underwear – oh no, this stuff was for the depraved, the deviants, the perverts... it had to be used underwear. This idea actually got given a lot more of a chance than the others, and I even went so far as to start investigating it online – it turns out weirdos like to be able to smell the 'aroma' of a lady on the underwear, and so there was no faking it – they had to be worn. Trouble was, as you've probably gathered by now I wasn't exactly turning away lines of women outside my door, and so finding one who was prepared to give me their dirty underwear on a regular basis was going to be a hell of a lot harder than finding one who was prepared to give me their phone number. But then I had a lightbulb moment - these mentalists wouldn't know who had worn the underwear, it could be Sophie from the halls of residence, Hayley from number 45, or Peggy from the old people's home round the corner. Equally, it could be me, Tom from Newbury... and so the plan was afoot!

Finding a pair of my ex-girlfriend's knickers in a cupboard I decided I'd go for it – it was going to be the beginning of my (albeit depraved and unmentionable) money-making empire. I have to admit, I did feel a huge pang of shame as I caught a glimpse of myself in my bedroom mirror pulling on a pair of tiny pink knickers with 'eat me' written across the front in glitter, and hoped to God that I wouldn't be involved in a serious accident and find myself in A&E having my jeans cut off by paramedics...

Still, money makes people do all kinds of things, and so with my head hung in shame I pulled on my jeans, tucked my balls back in, and set off for my lectures. It was at this point I discovered a whole new respect for women who wear thongs... damn that was an awkward walk through the town centre. Now I'm sure a thong is fairly snug anyway between the ol' butt cheeks, but holy shit it was so tight on me it felt like it was trying to test my prostate... I ended up walking so slowly and with my arms slightly bent out in front of me as if I was nervously rollerblading that it must have looked like I had either shat myself or was high on drugs. Oh what I'd have given for either of those to have been the case.

Eventually I got to the lecture hall and went to find a seat in the room, which was tiered in the classic amphitheatre style. Being university and not many people keen to appear eager to learn, all the spaces at the back of the room were taken and so I was forced to gingerly step down the best part of 30 steps before I could find a row with a spare seat. Christ the chaffing up my arse was unbearable. How the hell do women do it?! Do they whack a shit-load of Vaseline between their cheeks before leaving the house or just grimace for the first few years until they're able to take the pain?!

Then came the really hard part – sitting down. Slipped discs, piles, hip replacements and post-birth tearing are all valid reasons for moving as slowly and tentatively as I did towards that seat. Having an ex-girlfriend's pink thong strangling your balls was not one of them. Hiding the shame, I stayed rooted to that seat for the rest of the lecture, bar the odd shuffle to adjust which testicle was having its blood supply cut off.

Lecture over, I needed to a) get out of there, and b) pee. That was going to be a whole new challenge. Hobbling into the toilets, I took my place in front of a urinal, unzipped my jeans and tried to get my old chap out. It was like wrestling with a snake. And before my wife and ex-girlfriends begin to piss themselves laughing and go "yeah right!" I'd like to state it was like wrestling a snake because of the fact it was impossible to keep hold of the damn thing without the thong pulling back and squishing it a million different ways. The elastic must have been the same kind they use to launch fighter jets from aircraft carriers. I had to try a range of manoeuvres. Pull it to the side? Nope. Pull it to the other side? Nope. Pull it down? Bingo! I was just about to feel the sweet release of emptying my ever-growing bladder when THWACK – the bastard thong somehow wriggled free of my grasp and snapped back to pinch my old chap between it and the zip of my jeans...

Yelping like a wild animal caught in a trap, I pushed the thong back down before losing my shit – I grabbed each side of the castrating-contraption and pulled with all my might, every fibre of my being working hard to rip the bloody thong to pieces. I imagined I looked like Hulk Hogan ripping his neon vest in half. To the other guys standing behind me in the toilet I must have looked like a madman tearing his meat and two veg apart whilst roaring maniacally. Surprisingly, it didn't rip – I didn't even manage to pull a single bit of stitching out. So that old lothario phrase of "I'll tear your underwear off with my teeth" is a load of old rubbish - you stand a better chance of actually tearing your teeth out. Dejected, I let out a little whimper as I accepted the fact I was going to have to shuffle into a cubicle and engage in the bizarre ritual of a sit-down wee before being able to take them off. Once removed, and with my genitals throbbing from all the abuse, I firmly scratched the used underwear idea from the list of ways to make money.

Later that day, though, it finally dawned on me – just get a bloody job! Ah yes, the words my Dad had been shouting at me several times a year since I was 16 were now finally making sense and ringing true. And so I started hunting the local student job boards for anything that ticked the three magic boxes – a) preferably didn't involve working when I was meant to be in lectures (I say preferable, as it definitely wasn't essential), b) didn't involve serious concentration, and c) kept interaction with customers to a minimum (there was every chance I was either going to be knackered, hungover, or just miserable that I wasn't out with friends). Eventually my hunting found the perfect role – an evening shelf stacker at B&Q.

Whilst the hours were pretty shit (8pm until midnight) this was the absolute dog's bollocks of jobs – there were hardly any customers around as the store shut an hour after I started and bar the insomniacs getting ready for a busy night of DIY and the weirdos trying to find somewhere to loiter for an hour or two, it was empty. Bliss! The job itself was a piece of piss – a stock check here, some tidying of the aisle there, interspersed with a fair bit of dicking around. Then once the shop shut at 9pm the hardcore night crew emerged from shadows – these were some crazy motherfuckers, more often than not doing the night shift because they were unable to deal with human interaction or in fact daylight. Pale as a ghost, and with dead but oddly twitchy eyes, I absolutely shit myself the first time I encountered the night crew, fearing that I was in fact mental and coming off my meds in some institution for the criminally insane, like Broadmoor.

As it turned out they were a lovely bunch! From Pete the geezer grandad who couldn't sleep and needed something to do, to Lizzie who was so sweet and lovely that she was working night shifts because it's all her husband was able to do and so she wanted to have a work and home life that was in sync with his, like a pair of loved up vampires. There was another young lad called Adam who started at 8pm and like me was a student, liked a beer, and loved to dick around. One night, before the night crew crazies came in, we were clearing up part of the warehouse when we found two random items in a clear bag on the floor. Looking like a pair of shiny metal plungers, they had a rod about the length of a finger attached to a thick disc about the size of a 10p coin.

"What the hell are they?" asked Adam.

"Damned if I know – let's have a look."

We were like warehouse magpies – curious about everything shiny and prepared to steal anything. On the side of the clear plastic bag was a sticker saying 'Bath magnets'.

"What the fuck are 'bath magnets'?" we both wondered out loud.

Keen to see what they were, we ripped open the bag like gleeful kids on Christmas morning, giggling and grinning from ear to ear. As I held them in my hands I started to move them closer together.

SNAP!

They clamped shut. Wow. It was impressive – they were at least 4cm apart still when the magnetic forces pulled them together.

"Ooooooh!" we both cooed, knowing there was some serious mischief we could get up to with these bad boys.

Trundling into the warehouse Pete saw us huddled together with our new toy and shouted over.

"Oi! What are you pair of fannies doing?"

Pete wasn't one for pleasantries.

"What you got there?" he asked, jabbing a bony finger towards us as he came closer, seeing we were trying to hide something.

"Nothing interesting, just a couple of *bath* magnets," replied Adam, emphasising the word bath to highlight the fact it was mad to think people had any kind of use for a magnet whilst taking a bath. I honestly couldn't think of what they could be for – was it to stick to a tap and make it easier to turn? Or maybe it was to stick to a metal plug and ensure you could pull it out when the bath was so full that the weight of the water made it feel like you were trying to pull a car off the bottom of the ocean floor.

"Oh, you've got yourself a couple of bath magnets there," he told us.

"Yeah, thanks Pete – that's what we just said."

"No, no, no – what I mean is, they're industrial-strength magnets that are used to hold a bath in place."

Ho-ly shit! We'd hit the jackpot! Adam I turned to one another, the biggest grins on our faces as thoughts of creating the kind of illusions that David Copperfield could only dream of filled our little minds. What would we do first? Stick them to the side of a van and create a seat to sit on? Pin a fiver to a manhole cover and watch people struggle to get it? A few hours later my shift ended and so did my enthusiasm for the public illusion ideas. Instead I found myself dicking around with them at home. After a few beers with my housemates we were curious about what they could squash with their force - we started with an ear lobe, which was suitably squashed to about 3mm thick, before graduating to other parts of my body... yes, my body, not theirs, so when talk inevitably turned to my crown jewels I immediately tried to calm the baying mob and offer up another body part.

"What about my nose?" I pleaded, "I bet that would be a good test!"

They groaned. After the idea of doing something with a penis is raised by a group of lads in their early twenties, nothing else will suffice. I was starting to worry they'd just pin me down and put the magnets on my old boy to get what they wanted, and with it having had a less than ideal amount of interaction with the opposite sex up to that point I really didn't want to bludgeon the poor thing to death before I had the chance to right that wrong. Quickly snatching the magnets from the lads I held them either side of my nose and, using all my strength to steadily guide them closer together and avoid them snapping shut, I placed one on each nostril.

My nose squished flat with an oddly satisfying squelch, looking, ironically, like a penis between two magnets. Turning to the guys, I went from having aspirations of David Copperfield to sounding like a weekend kid's party magician as I excitedly shouted "ta-daaa", the move complete with Panto-esque jazz hands.

Then it started to go wrong. I could feel the magnets moving ever so slightly as the sweat from my fear of being tortured by my nice but ruthless housemates trickled down my face and onto my nose. Deciding to tap out, I grabbed for the rods on each magnet, but I couldn't overpower the magnetic forces… yet another reminder I really should have gone to a gym more than twice a year…

'No, no, no, no…!' I squealed, as they slipped all the way down to the end of my nose before they clamped together with a metallic snap, nothing between them apart from a few molecules of sweat... and part of my nose. Anyone with the slightest grasp of physics and biology will be unsurprised to find that the soft flesh of the nose is no match for two lumps of metal, with the resulting pinch delivered as the magnets slipped off actually splitting the tip of my nose in between the nostrils. Now, I wouldn't describe myself as a manly man, and I doubt anyone who knows me would consider me that either, but even I was surprised at the squeal I let out as the magnets flew off my nose and the blood started to trickle down to my lips. Think Marv in Home Alone when the tarantula lands on his face, or Ned Flanders in The Simpsons when he kills his wife's plant. As I said, not very manly.

Cut yourself in most places on your face and there's normally a fairly manly excuse which can be dreamt up. Eyebrow? Clearly a fight. Lip? Another fight. Chin? Mountain biking down the side of a hill, or the old trusty go-to excuse of, you guessed it, a fight. But the end of your nose? Nope, there's no way to explain that one away. You can't claim a fight for that one. Shit, I thought, the guys in B&Q are going to take about two seconds to figure out what happened and that's it, I'll be forever known as the bellend who split his nose with a pair of magnets. I can't be having that, I remember thinking. Christ, it was bad enough being mocked for having the audacity to use hair gel when doing the nightshift, they would dine out on this mishap for years... the only thing to do was to keep my head down, literally.

I turned up for my next shift and decided the best way to avoid anyone noticing was to come up with a plausible excuse for why my head would be bowed down. I'd contemplated the options on the walk in - depressed? Possibly. But there might be a chance one of the old timers would take pity on me and try to take me aside for a proper chat. Looking for something tiny I'd dropped on the floor? Better, but I couldn't exactly keep that up all night long. Sudden onset of osteoarthritis? Bit of a stretch at my age, and given the fact quite a few of my colleagues looked like they were constantly auditioning for the role of the Hunchback of Notre Dame I was fairly sure they'd smell a rat right away. Maybe I was overthinking it? Nothing beats a good old 'cricked my neck during a nap' excuse. Plus they really wouldn't care less about a momentary injury like that and instead would offer such words of encouragement and sympathy as "Get on with it you fanny!" and "Stop trying to get out of work you lazy shit!" and pay me even less attention than normal. So the decision was made - a cricked neck it was.

Five minutes after starting, the ruse was working, and I walked up to Adam.

"You'll never guess what happened last night mate..." I started.

"I bet my night was worse," he replied.

Slowly looking up at me I was amazed to see he had a great big cut on the end of his nose too, right between the nostrils!

"The magnets!" we both cried out, laughing loudly before quieting down to avoid anyone coming over to see what was going on and figuring out what had happened.

So it turns out he'd also nabbed a pair of magnets and reached the same conclusion after a few drinks, opted for one of the less risky pieces of our anatomy to test them on, and so we'd both ended up in the same situation - frantically trying to stop them slipping off the end of our nose before the inevitable pinch, squeal and bloody shame took place.

Oh how Magnes the Greek shepherd must be rolling in his grave at the thought of how a couple of absolute plums like us were ruining humanity's penchant for finding incredible new ways to use the power of magnets for the greater good.

Faux pas 17

The blood blister

People will do all sorts of things to get some money in. Whilst I've never truly plumbed the depths of desperation for work (although attempting to wear women's underwear and sell it was a fairly low point in my life, which in itself is saying something considering I've shat myself in a public swimming pool...), I've had some pretty crap jobs in my time.

I had a single day's experience as a waiter. It was only a single day because halfway through my shift I ended up dropping an entire tray of champagne flutes whilst trying to serve a large group of people, and then tried to pick a shard of broken glass out of a diner's cleavage. Apparently, despite being helpful it was not acceptable, especially as I dived in wiggling my fingers. I have to confess, I was wiggling my fingers in the way that a bomb disposal expert might do before they dice with death as they try to disarm an explosive device, not like a sex pest about to get all handsy with a random lady's rack. But alas they didn't believe me - you see, I was only 17 years old. It's hard to disagree with anyone thinking a 17 year old making a play for someone's cleavage is for anything other than pure testosterone-fuelled joy, but I'll be honest the thought of touching a lady's breasts back then was equally as terrifying as the thought of potentially being sliced open by the glass. I was hardly a seasoned lothario who was looking to notch up another cleavage-conquest.

I was also a fishmonger for longer than I care to remember.

Hey, don't judge - everyone had a crappy job at a supermarket at some point growing up, right? I mean sure, not everyone was stuck behind a counter wearing a huge white overcoat, an apron and a little plastic hat... I looked like a proper bellend, and worse still I smelled horrendous.

"Wash your hands with cold water and soap," they used to tell me when I complained about smelling like a bloody fishing trawler for days on end after each shift.

Did it work? Did it fuck.

"You're doing it all wrong - wash your hands with cold water and soap and then rub them on the stainless steel sink," they then told me.

Did that work? In making me look like an absolute nutter who liked molesting sinks? Yes, I absolutely nailed that one. But I still managed to part a crowded bar when trying to get a drink after work like Moses parting the Red Sea.

The job did have its perks, though - hardly any customers wanted to buy fish and the fish counter was in a corner of the supermarket that management rarely ventured to, which meant that I was often free to read a magazine, message friends on my phone, cheekily eat the food on the counter and generally laze about. I admit, being able to eat the food wasn't a great perk when faced with fish, fish or more fish, but hey, after seven hours, some smoked mackerel or crayfish was not to be sniffed at. One shift at Christmas I was royally fucked off with having to wait two days before being able to go out with my friends into town to drink and try and meet girls without the fear of one of them thinking Captain Birdseye had rocked up. So I decided to calmly walk round to the bakery counter, grab a bag of doughnuts, then head to the booze aisle and grab a bottle of Kahlua, and then waltz back to my fish counter and devour the lot. That was a great shift - although being tipsy and riding the sugar-high whilst trying to cut fish with razor-sharp knives was not a winning combination…

I remember a time when I had to do the morning shift on a Saturday but had been invited out for a night on the town by friends on the Friday.

"You'll be fine, just have an Ibuprofen and a pint of water before bed," they told me.

That might've worked if I'd only had four pints, went to bed at midnight and started work at 9am. But I'd drunk an obscene amount, gone to bed at 4:30am and had to start work at 6:30am. Who the fuck wants to buy fish at 6:30am?! Even the pensioners who hustled security to open the doors bang on time like it was Black Friday wouldn't buy any fish until the end of their shop. I could've rocked up at 8:30am and nobody would've noticed.

Instead, my alarm went off at 5:30am as I needed time to snooze it, have breakfast, get showered, get dressed and walk to the supermarket (the joys of being young, broke and healthy enough to walk anywhere on a whim). I could barely see straight. It didn't bode well. By the time I rolled into the supermarket (bang on time I might add - yay for me) I was not in a fit enough state to even talk to members of the public, let alone cut up a huge chunk of tuna or a whole salmon. Which is what I had to do, in order to make the nice fanned out display of tuna and salmon steaks on the bed of ice for the counter's display. We had these little blue plasters to use on any cuts we had. Nobody else ever cut themselves at work, they were mainly to use for scrapes and nicks people got outside of work, so we could remain hygienic in the workplace. Hell, even I never cut myself whilst working. But that morning, my oh my. The old hand-to-eye-coordination was well and truly gone. My hands, body and eyes were about as steady as a junkie in the final throes of withdrawal. In the time it took to cut one 12" slab of tuna into 1" steaks, I'd cut all four fingers and the thumb on the hand holding the tuna. I ended up looking like a Michael Jackson wannabe with all the finger plasters I ended up rocking. A stinking, ridiculous looking wannabe, trapped on a fish counter no less.

I also once managed about four hours as a Marketing Assistant. But to be fair to that shitshow, I was properly duped. They put an advert on a job website making it sound like it would be the kind of role you expect when you read the words 'marketing' and 'assistant'. So you can imagine my suspicion when they said at the start of the interview that they wanted to see if I would like to give the role a go by shadowing their current Marketing Manager for the day, and proceeded to then walk me out to a minivan to join several other people. It turns out the complete shysters were just doorstep chuggers (charity muggers, for the uninitiated) and soon we were being bundled out on the other side of town and given coloured bibs with the charity name on, a clipboard with direct debit sheets on, and told to come back in eight hours. My jaw hit the floor.

"Erm, what the hell is going on?" I asked.

"Don't worry," said the manager, "you'll be fine, you've

just got to embrace it and play the numbers game."

"I'm not knocking fucking doors. This was advertised as a Marketing Assistant role."

"I know, I'm sorry about that, but it's what the Boss wanted to do to get more people in."

"Well fuck this, I'm not interested. Can you take me back to the office, please?"

"Sorry mate, the minivan won't be back for at least another six hours."

"Are you honestly getting any success with this?" I asked, getting more incredulous that anyone was expected to make a living off of this.

"Yeah, and you have a right laugh, too! I once got chatting to this woman who was just wearing a dressing gown and she invited me inside and we got down to business in her lounge before I got back on with my shift! There's some proper crazy stories from people doing this."

I very much doubted it. Even if his shagging-a-random-lady story did happen, I think he left out the details of how many teeth she had and how many drinks she'd knocked back by the time he knocked on her door.

In the end he refused to call the minivan back early or offer me any kind of alternative transport, and so being all out of options I walked an hour back to the side of town we'd come from, and eventually managed to head home.

Wankers.

But the job that gave me some of my best and worst moments has to be labouring. Well, technically installing windows, doors and conservatories. It was a lifeline given to me by the owners of the company who knew I was shit out of luck after university in trying to find a job, and I was massively grateful - even if sometimes the danger level was higher than I'd hoped for.

A prime example of the everyday danger and risk of injury was when we had to replace someone's rickety upstairs window. It was so old we couldn't remove the pane of glass in one piece, so it had to be smashed out. Knowing the lady who owned the house had young kids, the decision was made to try and contain the broken glass as much as possible, as the window was above the garden. Perhaps it was a form of hazing as I was the new guy, perhaps it was because they didn't like me, or perhaps they just thought it was the best way to do it, but either way I ended up stood 20 feet up a ladder outside, wearing safety specs and gloves, holding a bucket and trying to catch the glass as good ol' Pete stood inside swinging a bloody hammer at the window pane. Yes, you read that right - I had to catch the fucking glass! Lunatics.

But I did love it - I mean, where else could you get paid to demolish things with pneumatic drills, sledgehammers and crowbars, gorge yourself on tea and biscuits, listen to the radio and have non-stop banter? Every day was different, full of laughs and left you with tales to tell - stick that in your pipe, shitty office jobs.

Some incidents, however, were near-death experiences that

I never wanted to experience again. Like the time I had to help manoeuvre the roof glass into place for a conservatory that had been built over a swimming pool, only the pool was empty and I was standing on a ladder balanced on a couple of scaffolding boards extended across the pool… Or the time when we were replacing a wooden bay window and needed to use an electric reciprocating saw to cut through the posts. If you don't know, a reciprocating saw is basically a long blade with jagged teeth like a handsaw which is connected to a giant drill that then rapidly moves the blade back and forth, so you don't have to move your arm to saw something - the motor does the hard work. We were conscious that the solid chunks of wood forming the bay window could fall into the customer's lounge and damage their furniture (they had already given us a warning not to let sawdust get on their furniture or tread on their flowers underneath the bay window) so we decided that the best thing would be for me to hold my arms out, ready to catch the posts once Pete had cut through them.

The trouble was, the roof of the bay window weighed more than we thought and was pushing down on the posts, pinching them tightly in place. We should've just got one of the ceiling support props we had in the van which were specifically designed to hold a roof up, but instead Pete, an old school cockney who favoured brawn over other options, went for an angled cut on one of them and leaned into it with all his weight, the reciprocating saw straining as the blade fought against the compression of the wood as it slowly made its way through.

As the blade emerged victorious from the post, our faces barely had time to switch from strained-concentration to delight, because they were instead forced to convey sheer horror as Pete's force caused it to continue moving well past the post and sink itself into my outstretched arm… the bastard thing ended up sawing across the inside of my elbow joint, catching several veins in the process. Not pretty.

The bollocking from the customer was for some reason the first thing I thought of, as I desperately gripped my arm with all my strength to stem the bleeding - if they were ready to go apeshit at some sawdust on a coffee table, imagine their reaction to a pint of claret dripped all over their carpet?! Tottering outside, I then decided to try and channel some of Pete's old school attitude and wrapped my arm up with a rag we had for cleaning and told him "Let's crack on with the job!" as I thought I could go to hospital after I'd helped him put the new bay window in. He questioned my decision, but ultimately supported it as finishing up on time would've allowed him to get home to watch the Chelsea game. We switched places so I was outside and he was inside cutting the other post, but I lasted about five minutes before the rag was soaked through and I was dripping blood all over the lawn, and so we decided to get me taken to get patched up before I passed out.

Other incidents were pure comedy, like fucking up my first experience of pushing a wheelbarrow full of cement from a mixing truck to the massive trench which had been dug for the foundations of an extension - I not only failed to prevent the wheelbarrow falling in when I tipped the cement in, but I proceeded to wail like a banshee as I foolishly clung on and got dragged down with it into several feet of sloppy cement.

Or the time I was replacing the windows at a big burly firefighter's house and went to use the toilet only to find a photo on the toilet wall of said firefighter in his formal work shirt, a pair of pants and thigh-high high-heeled leather boots. Erm... Emerging from the toilet more than a little scared for my personal safety, I scurried back to the van and asked Pete what the absolute fuck was going on.

"Didn't you know?" he asked. "His family ran a shoe factory that was struggling to survive, and the only way they could stay afloat was to diversify, and so they saw a gap in the market for transvestite footwear and it went wild. They even made a film about it."

It turned out that I had stumbled upon the family who the movie Kinky Boots was based on! Thoroughly lovely people they were, too.

Then there were the awful ones, like finding dead animals trapped in walls, people who clearly couldn't look after themselves and had toilets and sinks black with filth built up over the years (the tea they made us was instantly launched into the bushes as if we were handling Novichok), or the couple who left soiled underwear for us to move to get access to windows and let about 20 cats roam their house and piss everywhere without cleaning it up, which made working in there in the middle of summer comparable to a stint in Guantanamo Bay.

There was even one time where I had to superglue some decorative caps on to the ends of the windowsill we'd just installed, but in my haste to make sure the fiddly bastard things stayed in place I used way too much superglue and actually ended up gluing several fingers to the windowsill.

I was well and truly stuck, and the bastards on site did nothing to help me. Instead, they left me, and as the afternoon wore on they threatened to get in the van and drive home, leaving me there unless I escaped. It wasn't exactly the nicest part of town, and so fearing my arse would become a fairground attraction for an opportune rapist if left there overnight, I closed my eyes, thought of keeping my anus intact, took a deep breath and ripped my hand from the windowsill. I can still remember the tearing sound. Awful business. My fingers hurt like hell and the top layer of skin was still stuck to the plastic frame, but I was free and heading home so you know, all's well that ends well.

To be fair I'd have pissed myself laughing too, like the time Dave sat down for lunch on a toolbox and knocked a pot of superglue over as he did it, yet somehow didn't notice until he had finished his sandwich and read the paper - a whole hour later. As he stood up the toolbox came with him, and after much hilarity we realised there was no way to detach the toolbox without force… and so like someone carrying out an amputation in a field hospital during the US Civil War, Pete gave him a wad of tissue to bite down on, and then proceeded to rip the toolbox from his arse. Amazingly two patches of his boxers and trousers refused to detach, and it was too painful to try any more ripping shenanigans so the poor bastard got Pete to cut around the patches and was forced to let them grow out. Imagine that, walking round for weeks with two patches of fabric on your arse cheeks? We later learned that there were of course solutions that could be applied to lessen the grip of the glue and allow the little fabric patches to harmlessly fall off, but I'm glad he didn't realise!

Like I said, every day was different.

I loved the adventure, and the ability to flip between using delicate skills one minute and power tools the next was addictive. Only two things scared me - angle grinders and circular saws. I never understood how the guys could laugh about all the horrendous injuries they'd heard about from other tradesmen, but from those stories I learned to have the utmost respect for those power tools, because without it I'd end up losing a finger, a hand or worse.

Eventually came the day where I was faced with handling one of the beasts. It was early December and I had been tasked with using a circular saw to shorten all the long pieces of wooden window and door frames we'd ripped out over the last few weeks, ensuring they were cut into pieces small enough to fit inside the owners' log burner to keep them toasty in winter. Knowing that I needed to keep my hands away from the blade as I was lowering it down to cut through the wood, I was meticulous in my handling of both the saw and the wood.

All was going well and I was working my way through the huge pile of wooden scraps, but holy crap it was boring - whilst the other guys were out enjoying another adventure I was instead standing in a freezing cold yard cutting piece after piece of wood. Obviously I tried to speed things up. I decided to pull the saw down and cut through the wood quicker and quicker each time. What I didn't realise, as I'd been given just the basic instructions of "Turn it on like this, cut like this, and don't chop your bloody fingers off" was that as sharp and fast as the blade was it wasn't magic and it could easily snag on the wood. What then happens is the blade stops, but only because it's been gripped by the wood. What I also didn't realise was that this would cause the piece of wood to flip over.

The end result of this was that the piece of wood I was cutting did indeed snag and then rapidly flip, pinching one of my fingers against the metal base of the saw unit as I tried and failed to hold it in place. And that, ladies and gentlemen, hurt like hell.

Killing the power to the saw I was able to lift the wood up and release my finger. It was immediately turning dark red as a massive blood blister started to appear. Now, I'd had a few blood blisters in my time, but they were only diddy little things from being nipped by a chain when fixing my bike. This was a beast - it covered the entire end of my finger, and was soon bulging so much it looked like it was E.T.'s.

Keeping it a secret from the managers so that they wouldn't know what a complete muppet I was, a week later I found myself at the company Christmas meal. Heading to a local restaurant with the team, their partners and the co-owners it had started to turn into a nice evening, despite the eclectic mix of personalities present - a carpenter, a martial arts fanatic, a former sailor, a businesswoman and Pete the Chelsea geezer extraordinaire. Given that list you'd assume it'd be odds-on that something would go awry, right?

As the drinks started flowing, the laughter ramped up and we started to make our way through the feast laid on for us. Getting to the main course the co-owner sat opposite me was excited as the waiting staff started bringing out even more dishes of sumptuous food. Catching a glimpse of my odd-looking finger she asked me what happened.

"Oh this? I had a bit of a scare with the saw in the yard the other day…"

"Oh my goodness, are you alright?" she asked, genuinely interested in my wellbeing.

"Yeah, I mean I was lucky as it could've been worse, but I tell you what - this blood blister is killing me."

"Oh my word," she exclaimed as she caught a glimpse of it.

"I know, right?"

"Mind you," she said, studying it intently, albeit from the other side of the table, "I've seen some horrible blood blisters over the years, and thankfully that one doesn't look too turgid."

What? Not turgid enough? Well I wasn't about to let the fanfare die down so soon after my injury had been unveiled. I was hoping for a little more sympathy or banter than that. I decided I'd show them how bad it really was.

"Well it may have gone down a bit since last week, but I tell you what," I said, squeezing my finger to restore the blister to its former turgid glory, "it was ridiculous - look at it, it was like this all week."

And with that, she leaned forward at the precise moment it burst.

In any other circumstances I'd have laughed. Hell, she might have laughed. But absurdly it hadn't burst in the traditional sense - oh no, it was just a tiny pinhole that had appeared in the skin - and under all that pressure caused by me squeezing the damn thing, the blood shot out of the end like a SuperSoaker. Everyone watched in horror as this jet of blood shot over the table onto her pristine white blouse, before trailing off all over her freshly served Christmas dinner.

There were no words. Just a look of "oh fuck" on all our faces, mine especially.

Learning from the previous debacle with the broken glass champagne flutes as a waiter I decided this time to do nothing, which in hindsight also wasn't great as I ended up looking like a complete arsehole who had just squirted blood all over his boss' clothes and dinner and then just sat there watching her freak out and try not to wretch as Pete handily suggested she just "eat around it". What a legend.

And so it came to pass that never again would I sit near either of the co-owners at any future company celebrations. I think it's safe to say that was a good call.

Faux pas 18

The headphones debacle

Earphones. They are arguably one of life's greatest inventions (admittedly behind things like the wheel, computers, penicillin and the NHS). Every day they provide millions of commuters, students, bored workers and audiophiles the ability to experience everything from the finest details to the deepest bass of their favourite tunes, all without disturbing those around them.

Of course, there are some who reject the fabulous concept of polite music listening and instead choose to infect our ears with their utterly shit blend of 'music' to the point where regular people daydream about taking a big swing at the side of their head with a spade, followed by several swings to the offending device blasting out the tunes. Yes, we are talking about all the people who feel compelled to sit, walk or cycle around with their phone (or even a portable speaker, the absolute parasites) blaring out tunes for all to hear. I don't believe these people search online for 'mobile phone' or 'portable speaker'. I think they look for 'hate-attracting device', 'speaker most likely to result in me being bludgeoned to death' or even 'how can I become even more of a bellend?'. As you can tell, I'm not a fan.

But one of the other massive benefits of earphones is that you can readily watch videos without alerting your friends/commuters/colleagues as to the content of said videos. Yes, I'm skirting around the issue, but you all know I'm talking about that wonderful thing known as porn.

Whilst pretty much every male I know is an avid fan of pornography, and some females too (big shout out to my friend Georgina who at school let me stash a porn magazine at her place, only for it to be returned a few weeks later with a lot of well-thumbed pages), I think it's pretty much just us guys who appear to share videos of all kinds of depravity over WhatsApp. Not a day goes by without someone I know sending me a video of something featuring boobs, bums and a smattering of dicks. Mostly it appears to be funny content, like a couple having sex in the most ridiculous place and either falling over or getting caught. Some is just bizarre, such as the guys getting their Crown Jewels pummelled by naked midgets, and some of it is, well, let's just say it often gets deleted as soon as the thumbnail image pops up. But before some Crown Prosecution Service jobsworth starts salivating at the prospect of confiscating my phone and taking me down, I don't mean illegal stuff - I mean depraved stuff, like a lady pushing an entire pack of frozen sausages out of a place they really shouldn't have been squeezed into. Like I said, depraved, but not illegal.

Incidentally, there's a story there from my life outside work, where as a teenager I was at a friend's house party and things were getting pretty wild as they do when teenagers are exposed to mid-strength lager and drinks containing more sugar than alcohol (I'm looking at you Smirnoff Ice and WKD). It was well into the evening of a BBQ and drinks session when all of a sudden there was an awful smell in the air and people started shrieking in horror. Thinking that someone had fallen onto the BBQ and turned themselves into KFC I considered how best to go and help the human Zinger burger before teenage nonchalance kicked in and I returned to my sickly-sweet alcopop and carried on talking to a friend. I really should've paid more attention.

Mere moments later I was mid conversation when what has gone down in folklore as "the shit burger" was thrust in my face. Much like when someone gets sucker punched (for the uninitiated it's a cheap shot where someone gets punched from behind so they don't see it but feel the full force of it, usually knocking them out) it was launched from behind and I took it to the face. It later transpired that Eddie, the motherfucker who did it, had actually taken the grill off the BBQ, crimped off a length, and then returned said grill to the BBQ to charr it off. Talk about commitment. So it really was a shit burger. Well, shit hotdog to be precise.

It's one thing to have shit on your face. It's another thing entirely to have burning hot shit on your face. Coupled with the fact it was done in front of dozens of other teenagers, I'm sure you can appreciate how utterly mortifying it was.

Not one to accept being made to look a fool, I immediately gave chase, trying desperately to catch the bellend who did it and beat the shit out of him. But alas the fucker was faster than me, and so I gave up and decided an alternative approach to ensure I got my revenge… and that is when I went and cleaned myself up, picked up the remaining shit burger, and then proceeded to walk into the lounge of his parents' house and covered their wallpaper in the still-smouldering shit.

As people gasped in horror at my dirty decorating, I became enraged that they thought shit in the face was fine but shit on a wall wasn't. It was only as I was getting ready to storm out of the house that I heard someone ask "Why the fuck is he doing that to Matt's parents' lounge?"

Matt? Oh no... It appeared that in my drunken state I'd forgotten we'd actually gone round to Matt's house, not Eddie's, and so I'd ended up smearing shit across a perfectly innocent family's walls. At that point I switched from storming off to sneaking off, and hoped that Matt didn't find me anytime soon!

Anyway, getting back to the earphones, another phenomenon is the porn-audio prank. I feel like everyone has been caught out by this one at some point, or knows someone who has, but if by some miracle you're yet to get taken down by it, this is the trick where you send a seemingly innocent video to your friends but at a certain point the audio switches to a lady moaning the kind of moan reserved for childbirth and porn (but not real sex, or so my wife assures me...). Even if the volume on your phone is set to low in the anticipation of such a prank, it still seems to echo throughout every office/train/bus and lead to the kind of judgement from other people you thought would only be reserved for those flashing/urinating/vomiting in public.

Fully aware of the tendency of my friends to try and catch me out with this kind of prank, I often set my media volume to off when I'm on the train or in the office. On this particular day, though, I thought I'd just plug my work headphones into my phone and so be able to still enjoy the audio of some genuine videos such as the ones my wife would send me of my little girl playing at the park, and be safe in case my friends tried to catch me out.

But ah yes, it appears I've glossed over a tiny little detail here - my job involved making most of my calls over Skype using a little headset which could connect to any device via its audio cable, which meant it was easy to switch between plugging into my laptop for calls and into my phone for listening to music or videos. On this fateful day I decided I would be doing just that - switching between my laptop for the various monotonous calls with finance and HR, and my phone for a dose of Spotify and the occasional video from my family.

By 2pm I'd reached my daily limit of corporate bullshit, and so decided to check out the videos I'd been sent on WhatsApp. First up, a video from my Mum, of my Dad taking the dog for a walk. Next up, a video from a friend of the crowd cheering at a football match he was at last night. Finally, it was a video from one of my neighbours.

He was super friendly and polite, with our banter never straying beyond the shit Dad jokes everyone over 60 seems to love. It was a seemingly innocuous video of a group of guys telling jokes, but I noticed how the sound was pretty quiet and I wanted to hear the punchlines which were causing them to crease up with laughter. Knowing I was protected by the safety of my earphones I cranked the volume right up.

But something still wasn't right. Turning the volume up to full blast I was dumbfounded as I tried to work out why the audio I could hear was only increasing ever so slightly. Then I heard it. It was still faint but instantly recognisable - the ridiculous moaning of a porn star. Damn it, I'd been lured in and hit by the porn-audio prank.

One by one though, my colleagues lifted their heads from their laptops and stared in my direction. Oh for fuck's sake... Yep, not only had the bastard got me hook line and sinker with it but the worst thing had happened - I'd left my earphones connected to my laptop and foolishly thought I'd switched them over to being connected to my phone...

What. A. Muppet.

Not since I was six years old and got caught weeing in a pencil case had I gone this red with embarrassment... but at least this time I was able to laugh it off and claim I'd been stitched up by my friends - you can't quite do that when you're gleefully filling up your He-Man pencil case with piss!

"Oh for fuck's sake," I exclaimed loudly, hoping people would put two and two together and realise it wasn't my fault and that I wasn't actually watching filth in the workplace like a disgraceful little pervert. After that, I learned to minimise the risk altogether by not watching any videos at my desk whatsoever, although I would occasionally watch them in the toilet. Although this was also doomed to fail, because whilst I relied upon muting the videos as soon as they started it doesn't take a genius to figure out this can easily go wrong too.

Various studies have been carried out into the ability of the human brain to process and retain information at any given time. The latest findings indicate that we are able to hold between five and nine things in our minds at once, and if we try to process or think of any more than that we end up ejecting one to make way for the latest thing, leading to the situations where we simply forget something we really should've remembered. Put simply, it's why Post-It notes are the saviour of modern society.

And this, ladies and gentlemen, is what caused my downfall once again with workplace video viewing, for on the next occasion it went wrong I really should've remembered the basics of 'make sure the video is muted', but I can only imagine the pressures of work led to me trying to think of 10 things at once and the 'video muting' thought got ejected into the ether of my mind...

It was a fairly typical day, however it was punctuated by a fairly unusual situation - I needed to use the toilet for a number 2. I say this was unusual because I'm a regular as clockwork 6:30am kind of guy when it comes to that area. And I genuinely mean it - many a time I've rued my body's reluctance to deviate from this. There's nothing worse than not being able to sleep off a hangover, have a lie in or continue to soothe the baby and let your partner sleep because your bowels are a stricter timekeeper than a Japanese train conductor.

So whilst it was most unusual, it was also most frustrating, because whilst I'd 'been summoned' by the feeling down below, once I'd settled down onto the toilet there was nothing, no activity whatsoever. Now I don't know what kind of toilet loiterer you are, but I'm fairly certain there's three kinds: those who love to read a good bit of printed text; those who love to have a bit of screen time courtesy of a mobile or tablet; and then there are those oddballs who just like to stare into space, focussing their mind on the task at hand and becoming zen-like until the deed is done.

Personally, I hate the idea of reading anything like a book - fucking hell, just imagine all the germs getting in between the pages... Has anyone ever swabbed second-hand books before buying them to see what is growing on them? Much like the tests you read about where scientists swabbed a number of door handles and handrails to see how many germs were being unwittingly picked up by various people, I have no doubt if someone swabbed the pages of a second-hand book they would find it as rife with disease as the floor of a toilet cubicle in a nightclub. I shudder at the thought...

Equally though, I'm not one for focussing too much (you might've picked up on that theme in this series of confessions) so I'm left with the option of catching up on messages or watching videos on my phone. This time, I received a video from a friend that looked like it would be someone about to attempt a trick shot whilst playing snooker blindfolded and with parts of the table on fire. Pretty batshit crazy I think you'll agree, and worthy of having a watch whilst I waited patiently for business to conclude. Alas, it turns out it was all just a ruse, for as soon as I had hit play I was faced with the kind of sex noises which could only be described as 'farcical' - nobody in their right mind would make those kinds of noises, not even in the fake and exaggerated world of porn. No, this was like the scene in 28 Days Later when the animal activists break into the lab full of raging chimps and the audio that greets your ears can only be described as psyche-splitting.

Cue blind panic. My eyes, wild with fear, looked around the cubicle for something, anything, to muffle the noises coming from my phone. My fingers weren't working as I flailed about trying to stop it, the simple act of pressing the volume buttons too much for the clunky slabs of meat I called my hands. Trying to find anything else which could make a noise to disguise the soundtrack of raging chimps/rutting pornstars, I panicked even more, and attempted a bizarre and feeble array of actions to create more noise - from kicking the edge of the cubicle wall to coughing as loudly as I could... It barely sounds plausible as I write it now, but because of the fact that in my haste I tried all of these things at the same time, I actually ended up sounding like I was having a seizure and no doubt drew more attention to myself. Bollocks.

There was definitely someone outside the cubicle finishing up washing their hands. They'd not used the hand dryer though. They were clearly listening intently to figure out if I was dying and they needed to go and seek the help of a first aider. Which in our office, all nine floors and 3,000 people of it, meant a tannoy announcement would be made across the entire building for a first aider to make their way to the location of need, resulting in about 10 people with medical bags descending on the male toilets in about 90 seconds if I didn't defuse the situation! The only thing for it was to follow up with the kind of noises which would leave them in no doubt that what had just happened was in fact just a furious emptying of my bowels and there was nothing else to be concerned about - bar how quickly they could escape the toilet.

And so, with great shame (also tinged with great pain) I quickly focussed my mind and unleashed fury. Thankfully, it got the job done and saved my embarrassment, but it also left me wondering - in the world of espionage, has any agent had to shit on demand to keep their cover from being blown? If not, MI5 - you know where to find me.

Faux pas 19

Deep-bedding gone wrong

In the workplace, or most environments where you're not alone or exclusively in the company of close friends (or spouses for that matter), breaking wind is taboo - whether it be a little 'pffft' that barely registers on anyone's radar, a ripper which is picked up on the Richter scale, or something more aromatic which makes you claw the walls and try to prise open the nearest window to avoid suffocation.

A lot of the time workers utilise cunning means of disguising the act, from the simultaneous cough to mask any noises to 'deep-bedding' it into the upholstery of a chair to prevent any aromas escaping and ending up in the nostrils of colleagues. It's commendable effort, although there's nothing more hilarious than someone mistiming their cough and simply drawing attention to themselves just as their arse sets off like a brass band. The real upstanding members of the office will make their excuses and venture into the toilets to release their backside banter. I think as you get older you tend to give less of a shit, as has been perfectly displayed by Alan, a wily 50-something engineer who is happy with everything in life and counting down the years to retirement. Alan likes nothing more than occasionally dropping a little ripper which sounds like someone starting up a petrol lawnmower or chainsaw. It draws equal amounts of smirks and admiration from the males in the office as it does frowns and disgust from the females.

For me, the aromatic ones tend to be quite rare things, like not getting drunk at a wedding or having spontaneous sex once married with kids. And as grim as it is, we all know that sometimes certain combinations of food and drink the day before will result in the need for HazMat suits to be worn by anyone in the vicinity the following day, like we're cooking up meth or handling chemical weapons. I defy anyone to load up on red wine and oily foods and not end up retching after dropping a real beauty the next day.

Funnily enough, on the day this incident occurred, I was coming off the back of a particularly gastric-testing weekend: all-day drinking on the Saturday followed by litres of red wine and some roast beef gluttony on the Sunday. It was written in the stars that Monday was going to be challenging...

Knowing that one ill-timed release could trigger pandemonium and authorities being called in to deal with a suspected chemical incident, I employed the mix of politely using the bathrooms for my sinful releases along with deep-bedding into my chair when I was stuck on calls and unable to leave my desk. It was working so well - I was smugly thinking I could make it all the way to 5pm and pull off a hell of a feat.

Stuck on a call late in the afternoon I was keen to avoid any more releases as the hot and uncomfortable feeling in my guts told me this would not be pleasant for anyone within 10m of my vicinity. We were in a 5m x 5m office, making it a certified kill zone. But try as I might, my organs conspired against me and I found myself having to deploy Operation Deep-Bed once more. Not long after, I caught a whiff of what can only be described as decaying matter with a hint of smoked paprika, and decided I needed to force my weight down into the chair even more to trap the filth in the cheap foam padding and retain my semi-professional reputation.

As soon as the call finished Gemma suddenly appeared by my side. Gemma was lovely, a genuinely kind and helpful person who'd only ever been nice to me, but always at arm's length. We were professional - colleagues but not outright friends.

"Hi Tom, can we talk about the report that needs to be sent before Friday?" she asked.

Startled, and momentarily forgetting the deep-bedding attempt, I turned slightly in my chair to glance at her.

"Erm, not right now, how about tomorrow?" I offered.

"Well it will only take a minute."

"It's really not a good time," I insisted.

"I'll be quick," she persevered. "So the figures we've put in the last table, I thought that they..." she began to quieten, before continuing, "...are not what we should be including at this stage but..." and she trailed off once again. Then I realised. Operation Deep-Bed had unequivocally failed, and the chemical warfare offensive was well and truly underway.

Looking at her with apologetic and sympathy-seeking eyes, encouraging her to please continue and overlook the fragrant assault on her senses, I slowly nodded and then tried a faint smile to let her know that it was okay, and that we should just continue without ever acknowledging what had happened. That together we could ignore the elephant in the room... but alas no, she couldn't do it.

Retching a little bit, before blowing the air out of her nostrils to protect herself from the aroma, she stared at me with cold eyes before walking away whilst saying "No, I'm sorry, I can't. I just can't," and left me to wallow in my own filth. The awkwardness was pretty intense. I struggled to hide my shame. Plus thanks to the risk of releasing more of the offending aroma into the office I also couldn't run away and hide. It was a bleak place to be.

Our relationship took a while to recover from that incident, although I could tell the disgust and contempt for me was never far beneath the surface afterwards. Which to be honest was completely fair. Since then I've made a point of trying to eat less red meat, drink less red wine, and generally be less of a reprobate when in the company of others. Apart from my dear wife – she gets nothing but the 100% genuine Tom experience, and for that I am forever sorry!

Faux pas 20

When the evidence is in plain sight

My reputation with my managers tended to follow a predictable pattern of rising, plateauing and then descending to varying levels after one or more incidents - be they unprofessional, performance-related or just downright unsavoury.

If I was to characterise the types of failings which went on to have the most impact on my reputation and career, I'm fairly certain lying is the big ticket item. Swearing in a meeting? Not ideal. Talking trash over the company intranet? Worth an informal chat. Using a permanent marker to make the 8ft high marketing images adorning the office hallways more hipster via some well placed moustaches? An informal warning. But lying? Well, that's actually one of the easiest ways to get HR buy-in for a formal warning, or even dismissal.

Being fairly young (although definitely old enough to know better) I was sometimes happy to finish early without necessarily seeking my manager's approval. The thing is, normally I'd have put in a 50 hour week before taking two hours off on a Friday afternoon, which wouldn't have been unreasonable. But on this occasion I'd not put in a long shift for some time, and yet I was fairly confident that whilst the lack of extra hours didn't necessarily justify the early finish, my quality of work did.

This was a throwback to my sales days where the mantra was "When you're bringing in the deals you can waltz in with your pipe and slippers and put your feet up," as the bosses wouldn't give you grief after doing such a good job. You'd earned the right to saunter round the office at a leisurely pace for a day or two. I don't think that sentiment is felt in engineering companies, however.

It was mid-afternoon on a beautiful day in June and I remember thinking that work was boring as hell and the weather was glorious, so I decided to wrap up and head home. The joys of our team was that my manager was based in another office about 80 miles away so as long as I kept my work mobile on me I could take his calls right away and keep up the appearance of still working. Even if he questioned why it was so quiet and there was no background noise, I was prepared - I'd simply throw out the classic answer of "I'm working from home!"

Top tip - nothing throws up a red flag more than calling your manager back 20 minutes after their call, then announcing you're working from home. That's the stuff of amateurs.

Thinking I was pretty savvy and that my boss wouldn't bother me, but with my work mobile on hand and ready to do emails via the mobile app should I need to maintain the pretence of being 'fully engaged', I packed up and headed home. Ah, it was pure bliss, driving back in the summer sun before changing into shorts and a T-shirt to get the garden ready for a BBQ with friends on the weekend.

After an hour or so of clearing the decking and scrubbing the BBQ clean (how can a grill go from moderately clean to looking like terrorists are growing some bioweapon on it within the space of a few weeks?!) I got a call. It was from my manager, Malcolm.

"Hi Tom, are you alright?"

"Yep, I'm fine thanks, are you okay?" I replied.

"I am, I just wanted to see if you were still able to work on that presentation for the quarterly meeting as I need the slides tomorrow."

Hmmm, must've forgotten about being given that action. Bugger.

"Yeah, absolutely fine Malcolm, I've got it all in hand," I fired back, then decided to throw in a bit of swagger. "I'm actually working on them right now, they're looking really good."

"Oh really?"

Hmmm, another curious question from no-nonsense Malcolm. What was he getting at? Then he hit the home run he'd just teed up perfectly with that teasing little quip...

"Only I've popped into the main office to get ready for the meeting tomorrow and can't seem to find you, and Emma said you left about an hour ago."

Alert! Alert! He's on to you! My mind was ringing with this rather unhelpful little sentence. It was clearly time to play the ace up my sleeve.

"Yeah I decided to finish it at home as the office was getting a bit too loud for me to concentrate."

That'll do it, I thought, smiling to myself as I tried to quietly make my way back into the house to at least try to sound like I was sat in my study, rather than have the whirr of my neighbour's lawnmower give the game away.

And then dear old Malcolm, no-nonsense but forever tactile, made his counter move in this game of chess. He was a prime example of someone who didn't need to bang a table and shout to cut someone down to size. Oh no, he was like a professional Jenga player (if the pieces were emotions and rationale), able to delicately slide the right pieces out quietly and efficiently to leave you making your own mistakes and crumbling right before him.

"Okay Tom, well I'm working at your desk for the rest of the afternoon so call me on your desk phone if you need to run anything past me, otherwise I'll keep an eye out for the slides first thing tomorrow morning."

And that's when it dawned on me...

It seemed as though the world came rushing in and my eyes widened, like in the movies when something dawns on the lead character with the kind of realisation so startling that it feels like everything is about to implode.

You see, whilst I could answer emails from my phone, there was no way for me to remotely log on to access the presentation from anything other than my work laptop. The exact laptop I'd only gone and left on my desk...

Well done Malcolm, you had seen my ace and laid down a full house, knowing full well that I wasn't working on the slides from home.

And so after an unnaturally long pause as I tried, and failed, to come up with a plausible excuse, he simply signed off with a casual "bye" - but not said like he normally did, oh no, on this occasion it was more of a "byyyyyeeeee". It was so long and drawn out that I could tell he he was smiling smugly in the knowledge that I'd been caught out and we both knew it. It was the kind of smug farewell that I'd sadly become accustomed to from my wife, who would often use it to end a conversation where we'd bickered about something and I was adamant I was in the right, but she knew full well I wasn't and that in about five seconds after we finished talking I too would come to that realisation.

And so, with my professional tail between my legs, I was forced to enact a plan which saw me creep back into the office that evening to pick up the laptop ('Exhibit A' in my trial of skiving off work) and then work into the early hours of the morning to ensure I finished the damn slides and thereby persuade Malcolm to call off the dogs (also known as HR) from tearing me apart for such blatant lying.

Cheats never prosper, they say. But there's no mention of liars - and that is because they are often cunning enough to avoid being caught. I am far from cunning though, and so from that day forward I decided to stop the bullshitting and play by the rules. Well, as best I could. What also helped keep me on the straight and narrow was getting a promotion which massively reduced any free time I had, and thus removed any future chances to enjoy a cheeky early finish in the garden.

Missing the illicit thrill of an impromptu bit of laziness or bending of the rules, I've since turned my attention to dodging chores and expectations at home instead. Mind you, it turns out I'm pretty shit at that, too - I'm forever getting caught watching TV instead of tidying the kitchen, taking a cheeky nap instead of ironing, or claiming I've changed the baby's nappy. It's hard to claim that last one though when they're in the jumparoo and creating a scene of pure horror, like some kind of shit-volcano erupting... in my defence I had no idea it was shitty nappy, I was just expecting it to be another wet one and couldn't be arsed to undo the million poppers on the babygrow. Whoever decided those tiny fucking poppers were a good idea on baby clothing was a sadist. There is nothing more frustrating than when you're in a barely-lit room at 3am trying to do up all the the bastard poppers, and yet despite lining them up perfectly they just won't 'pop' together - no matter how hard you squeeze them and swear under your breath. My masculinity dissolves within seconds. Just make them with zips you pricks!

Which brings me to my final thought - angry whispering is a skill and a half, but one that is only really mastered when you get married, have kids, or do both. I've lost count of the number of times I've angrily whispered "Go the fuck to sleep," when a baby just won't settle, or been on the receiving end of "Roll over, dickhead," after falling asleep in the middle of the bed before my wife got in. Fun times.

Faux pas 21

The Westminster screenshot

Across my career there's been a common theme of technology combining with my own stupidity to set up my downfall. But sometimes, on very rare occasions, I end up being stitched up or caught out through absolutely no fault of my own.

By now you're probably struggling to believe that could be the case, but trust me - it does happen.

One such event occurred back when I began to climb the ranks within the engineering firm, and as a result was given more and more opportunities to gain exposure to the upper echelons of the worlds we operated in - from attending workshops with Directors to media briefings with mainstream press, and even events with celebrity guest speakers. All good fun and a chance to hobnob with people who last earned my salary when they were 19, and used Michelin stars to choose places to eat like I used food hygiene ratings to judge where to get my takeaway. What was particularly interesting were the events at Westminster - for me it represented a world where money, status and power were the essential traits needed to operate, along with a healthy dose of petulance, backstabbing and one upmanship. It was a world I craved to be in! But having never been to a private school I was worried they would be able to smell the poor on me as soon as I walked into their hallowed grounds and immediately eject me.

On this particular day I was joining my boss in attending

an evidence-gathering session where MPs had invited companies from across several industries to attend.

"Please step through the security scanners," I could imagine the guard saying, before the inevitable BEEP BEEP BEEP would alert the grisly armed police officers to a potential threat.

"What have we got?" the supervisor would ask, peering at the security monitor.

"It's bad, Sir," the guard would exclaim, "he's been educated at a standard comprehensive school."

"Jesus Christ, hit the emergency button and call in the SAS!"

My fear wasn't always rational, I must admit.

Now if you're not familiar with what an evidence-gathering session entails, it is essentially where MPs and officials from various organisations sit around and berate each other in the name of trying to pin the blame on someone following some kind of debacle (or in anticipation of an upcoming policy decision). Not exactly edge of your seat stuff, but it is quite effective and at times necessary to keep things working and avoid a major incident. Kind of like sex after five years of marriage.

Fearing the poverty-sniffing capabilities of the security guards, I was a little jittery and overly friendly as I stepped into the airport security-like section that greets visitors, in the way that a boyfriend would first greet his new girlfriend's parents after she's told him her Dad used to be a boxer/bouncer/butcher.

I was greeted by a fifty-something security guard who had such dead eyes and a slow, couldn't-give-a-shit demeanour that I felt my fears were completely mislaid and I was going to sail through.

"Empty your pockets and take off your belt, and put your bag, jacket and cufflinks into the tray provided, and make sure all electronic devices are in a separate tray," the guard rattled off, said with such a monotone voice that I was pretty sure he hated himself a little bit more every time he said it, which was likely to be hundreds of times a day. Poor sod.

Wondering what led him to become the sad, soulless existence in front of me I quickly went through the motions and stepped through the scanner.

BEEP BEEP BEEP!

What the...? I could see him eyeing me with suspicion, and so to try and help him out and nudge him into thinking I wasn't a raving lunatic hell-bent on causing chaos, I offered a shrug of my shoulders and a raising of my eyebrows to leave him in no doubt that I had no clue what had set the alarm off. I was confident he'd buy it, as I'd been delivering this particular "Well I dunno," gesture with aplomb since I was a mere boy standing in front of a smashed car window, my slingshot and bag of marbles thrown into a nearby bush. Sorry about the Mondeo, Dad.

But alas no, he stepped towards me, a frown on his face. "Have you emptied your pockets?" he said with a sigh and a thinly-veiled air of contempt. I remember thinking Jesus, this guy must think I'm a complete and utter twa… ahhhh, shit. I patted both my trouser pockets with my hands whilst saying "Of course I…" and felt the unmistakable bulges of a phone, wallet and Mars bar. Turns out I'd been so nervous about the ridiculous prospect of them deeming me not posh enough to enter, along with the flurry of commands he'd given me, that I'd straight up forgotten to do the most basic action of any security check.

The look on my face was one of pleading for mercy, with a dash of sheepishness, and a hint of a smile at the ridiculousness of the situation. If you can't quite picture it, think of the face you'd pull after realising at 3am on a lads holiday abroad that you'd locked the only key inside your hotel room, or arriving at a musical festival and realising you'd left you and your girlfriend's tent on the bus. Got it? Yep, that's the one. I apologised a lot for those two mistakes by the way…

Regarding me with the same contempt you would have for someone farting loudly in public, he offered a terse "Go back and empty your pockets," before walking back to his dedicated spot in the amphitheatre of security.

Duly complying with his order I sheepishly emptied my pockets, ignoring the chuckles and tuts coming from those behind me in the queue who were patiently waiting to get through security, too. Stepping through the scanner once more, I closed my eyes and waited for the inevitable ringing in my ears… but it never came. Result! Smiling, and admittedly with a bit of swagger, I waltzed through to the end area and waited to collect the items I'd dutifully loaded onto the trays ready for x-raying.

One by one they trickled down along the conveyor belt. Belt? Check. Jacket and cufflinks? Check. Phone, wallet and Mars bar? Check. But where was my bag? Looking across at the guard stationed at the x-ray monitor, I saw him squinting at the screen before beckoning over the guard I'd just pissed off.

"Sir can you come over here, please," he instructed, a look of frustration spreading across his face.

Having no idea what could be encouraging them to beckon me over and inspect my bag in closer detail, I huffed and sauntered over, certain that they were now just aiming to make a mockery of me for my earlier cock-up.

As it turns out, there's actually quite a few items you're not allowed to take into Westminster Palace or the House of Lords - which I was coming to appreciate after being told to read the large airport-style warning board which said what can and can not be carried through security. Some of it I could appreciate, like gas canisters or matches, whilst some of it I felt was absurd, such as torches. Thing is, much like when a new partner/in-laws/company informs you how they do things, you never really tell them what you make of it, you instead just smile, nod and agree to tolerate the ridiculousness of it.

Maybe it was the extra coffee. Maybe it was the childish excitement and nervousness of being quizzed by guards when there were big burly men with machine guns mere feet away, or maybe it was just because I was yet to have the Mars bar I'd bought on the way in and my blood sugar levels were nosediving. Whatever it was, I have no idea what was going through my mind when I decided to get footloose and fancy free as they started to pull the offending items from my bag.

"A torch? You're joking right, what am I going to do - start having an impromptu rave in the middle of the place?" I asked incredulously, finishing it off with a little mock rendition of raving with some glow sticks.

They both gave me the 'are you out of your mind?' look. Fair enough really. I never could dance.

Next up, they pulled out a small metal chain and miniature padlock. Now this was genuine security equipment - they were issued by my company to help us secure our laptops to immovable objects whenever we stayed at a hotel or worked from a public place to prevent them getting nicked. The little padlock was also handy as it could be looped through the zippers on my bag to prevent pickpockets having a cheeky rifle through my belongings whilst I was stood in a queue at a random shithole, such as the tube in London or anywhere in Manchester.

"And what am I expected to do with that?" I asked.

"This," he started, pausing for dramatic effect, "this..."

Oooh, repetition - he's really getting into this, I thought. We've got ourselves a wannabe Thespian who's putting on quite the show for the ever-growing queue of people still waiting to go through security - the bulk of which I might add were now tutting away, rolling their eyes and generally showing me very little support. Plus I swear one even mouthed the word 'prick' at me.

"...could be used to lock the doors to one of the rooms or hallways," he finished, somewhat failing to nail the dramatic climax to that little speech. I could see why he was here and not on stage at The Globe.

"Why would I lock the doors? How would I benefit from that?" I challenged him.

"You could do all sorts of bad things to the people in that room," he fired back.

"Erm, have you seen the size of me," I said, gesturing up and down at my tiny frame. "What could I do?" I asked, holding out my child-like hands to exaggerate the point.

"You don't have to do anything directly, you could lock the doors and then..." he tailed off, nodding to finish his sentence, as if the nod was clearly spelling out the final words needed.

"Oh, right, I see," I replied, the penny finally dropping, "I could light a fire or even set off a bo-"

Now if there is a number one unwritten rule of any security checkpoint in any part of the world, it is you don't say the b-word. I guarantee if you want a priority-boarding pass to the finest security inspection area of any airport, just throw out the b-word. There you'll be guaranteed such a detailed examination of your private life it makes a mortgage application seem like a quick-fire question round in a pub quiz, and an equally thorough examination of your private parts (which I doubt is anywhere near as fun as half the guys reading that sentence are imagining it would be).

Thankfully I didn't finish saying the dreaded b-word, which ironically would have set off a chain of events akin to an explosion, but everyone knew what I was in the process of saying, and it triggered the kind of heads rapidly lifted and turned in one direction response that is normally seen in a wildlife documentary on meerkats. Machine gun-toting guards included. Shit.

Sensing this was going south very quickly, I offered a pathetic "I'm sorry," giving my best pleading and puppy-dog eyes look, but I too was no amateur Thespian and they weren't buying it.

"Just think carefully about where you are," one of them snarled.

"Right, er, yes, er, sorry about that, it, er, won't happen again..." I stammered, unwittingly doing my best Hugh Grant impression.

A few more unzips of my bag, a little more rifling, and then one of them looks up at me, eyes wide with astonishment, before asking me "Did you think at all about where you were going today?"

"Erm, I did this morning when I woke up," I offered, sounding like a lost little boy, and wondering what they'd found which had clearly riled them up even more.

"Then why the hell have you got this with you?"

Ah. Yes. I could see why they were getting a little frustrated. Forgetting to take your phone out your pocket is one thing, and carrying a chain and padlock is another. But the knife? Yep, there was no arguing with that one, only a complete fucking moron would try to waltz into Westminster Palace with a knife. I was going to protest that it was only a Swiss Army knife and extol the virtues of having such a practical piece of equipment on me when I realised the futility of it all.

It was at that moment I realised I could perfectly recreate the grimace emoji. Some of the people still waiting to go through security let out an "Ooooh" and one even laughed, the bastard.

"Right, you can see how this is a problem, can't you?" the previously dead-eyed guard said, clearly now energised by the whole debacle.

And so we spent the next five minutes playing out a scene witnessed in schools across the world - someone in a position of authority chastising someone who's wronged them, and then the chastised person apologising and wishing they'd hurry the hell up so the embarrassment would end.

And then, thankfully, it was over. Handed a ticket which listed all of my offending items, I watched as they were placed in yet another tray and stowed away in a locked cabinet. I wonder if security guards peruse tray catalogues and give the same "Ooooh" noises regular folks do with car/clothing/furniture catalogues? I felt a little pang of pride when I saw that in all the other trays there was only one item confiscated from others before me - but then again I couldn't help but feel that's probably the kind of attitude most of society's undesirables have in relation to their convictions and ASBOs, and so quickly ditched the pride and decided to hot-foot it into the main building.

Just as I was exiting the bastion of belittlement, I heard the unmistakable BEEP BEEP BEEP once more, and turned around to smugly observe another fool being shaken down and paraded as the muppet they clearly were in front of the other waiting guests. Bizarrely though, it was an old man - he must have been in his 70s, with white hair and a sweet smile, dressed in a check-print shirt and beige trousers. He looked like he could have been the grandpa from the Werthers Originals adverts of years gone by, or from the Pixar Movie 'Up!'.

Smiling sweetly and pulling the same shrug move I'd tried mere minutes earlier, he stood there and waited for the guard to come over. Rather than stomping over and chastising him for being such an idiot, however, the guard smiled back and sauntered over, exchanging pleasantries with the grandpa. Well that was double standards if I ever saw it! He literally did exactly the same as I did, yet was being given the softly softly treatment. Unbelievable. Now, I'm not the kind of guy who likes to see an old man taken to the ground cage-fighting style by the security services, but I'm also slightly bitter and easily riled, so I at least expected him to be frog-marched to the side of the room and vigorously patted down. Yes, I realise I am at times a pathetic person.

Slouched in the exit doorway and watching the scene in front of me with a face my dear father likes to describe as 'like a smacked arse' (I've always been intrigued as to how hard you'd have to slap an arse to make it resemble a face) I suddenly found myself standing upright and quietly muttering "Oh, hello," as the old man dutifully emptied his pockets and proceed to pull out something I couldn't quite see but whatever it was, it enough to make the guard open his eyes wide and the grisly armed guards perk up too.

Gingerly picking it up from the tray, the guard proceeded to hold it aloft for all to see. It was a razor-sharp kitchen knife. A bloody kitchen knife! Cue a chorus of "Ooooh" from the queue of people who were also transfixed on the bizarre scene unfolding in front of us. Now either terrorists were really scraping the barrel for recruits or this grandpa was seriously losing his marbles.

Fully expecting the guard to just smile and give him a ruffle of his hair whilst saying "Ah, you little rascal, what are you like, eh?" I was shocked (and admittedly a little pleased) to see him embark on the same routine he went through with me mere minutes earlier, giving the grandpa a good dressing down for all to see. Most people decided to give him some privacy and allow him to maintain his dignity by staring at the floor or suddenly finding something of interest in their pocket. I, however, stood there with my arms folded and a tight-lipped smile on my face, nodding with approval that this saccharine-sweet grandpa wasn't in fact being let off for his misdemeanour. I looked every bit like a football manager standing on the sidelines nodding in approval as the referee makes the decision to send off an opposite team's player for some minor infringement. Aka, a smug little shit.

But then the old man offered up an excuse for why he was carrying the blade the day he was heading into Westminster Palace, and it was the most middle-class, practical and admittedly sweetest reason he could have given. Still smiling and seemingly unfazed by the drama he was causing he simply said "Well, it's to cut up my apple when I have my cheese and crackers in the park later."

This drew a sympathetic "Awwwww" from the guests on the other side of the room, and I made a mental note to remember that excuse for the inevitable occasion in the future when I once again end up in a situation like this.

Breaking free of that drama I finally made my way into the cavernous grand hall of Westminster Palace, admiring the incredible architecture and statues adorning the staircases, before navigating the winding corridors to find the room we were meant to be in. As soon as I stepped into the wood-panelled room, with its church-like pues at the back for the minions and plebs (like me) and ostentatious leather chairs for the key speakers, I realised that this was every bit the world I had expected - from the unwritten rules of where to sit and how to act, to the snide comments and filthy looks at the slightest infringement of said unwritten rules. I absolutely revelled in it. Tutting at someone who asked where to hang their coat (despite having stuffed mine into my bag mere minutes earlier to avoid having to suffer the same embarrassment) I slipped effortlessly into the mindset of the Westminster folly - I was like a pig in shit.

I found my boss sitting at the back of the room and quickly sat down beside him.

"Ready for your first taste of politics at this level?" he asked.

"Absolutely," I fired back, throwing in a "thank you for the opportunity to join you," for good measure, always keen to both show appreciation and also engage in a little bit of brown-nosing. I never understood the hatred for brown-nosing. Alongside nepotism, it was the quickest and easiest way to succeed in life! Why hate efficiency?

As the room quietened down, the chairwoman kicked off proceedings, reminding everyone of the etiquette of the evidence gathering session (basically, keep your mouth shut unless invited to speak and absolutely all phones on silent) and that it would be streamed live.

Ooooh, I'd never been on TV before, let alone live-streamed! That meant one thing - I had to up my attempts to appear professional and under no circumstances reveal how bored I may be if the conversation took a turn for the worse. Which in that line of work, was a very real possibility. Considering I have at one time actually been paid to watch paint dry (you've got to love the chemical industry) that really is saying something.

Surprisingly, it wasn't the mind-numbing crock of shit I'd expected, and in between actually learning a few things there was even a cameo from a vintage Top Gear presenter. Plus we were treated to some wonderful put downs which took me back to being in the one upmanship bitch-fest that was secondary school.

Chair-person: "So, can you please tell us why it isn't possible to accomplish this in the timescales we've just mentioned?"

Responder: "Well... as I recently mentioned, we are focussing on delivering scheme A before we can re-assign resources and -"

The chair-person cut them off with a classic I'm bored as hell with your bullshitting look, lowered their glasses and then fired off a delightful barb.

"Yes, thank you, we've all heard at great length what you've been spending the last six months doing, but it would be nice if you could actually answer the question, don't you think?"

Clearly this was de rigueur for these types of sessions as nobody else batted an eyelid, instead they readied their pens/phones/laptops to capture the (hopefully) less-bullshitty response of the industry expert. Me being still wet behind the ears on all things Parliamentary-etiquette, however, I couldn't resist letting out a little chuckle at the muppet in front of me having a strip torn off him. The joy of being amongst bitchy veterans aiming barbs at one another and the other newbies trying hard not to draw attention to themselves is that the most my outburst drew was the odd raised eyebrow.

Feeling like I needed to recoup some professionalism, I had to employ a tactic so often used in those situations where you really don't care too much but you need to look engaged and an active part of proceedings, such as those boring-as-hell meetings or when you get stuck talking to an accountant at a party. It was a combination that never fails - serious face, slight frown, little nod now and then, a few slower than normal blinks to show you're taking it all in, occasional pursing of the lips and even a touching of the chin in an expression which hopefully conveys "Hey, I'm intrigued and totally into what you're saying," and not "Holy shit I wonder what will be left in the Boots meal deal by the time I get out of here?"

Actually, I really went to town with this approach, and by the end I felt that I was in a rhythm with it. Plus my boss didn't once stop me and say "Are you taking the piss?" so it was all good. In the end I survived, and once it wrapped up I was able to relax and revel in the fact that I was waltzing down the opulent hallways of the fine establishment, being every bit the proper tourist and taking photos of the decor. A stereotypical government official came out of a meeting room when I was stood taking a selfie with a statue and tutted at me, causing me to immediately lose my swagger and scuttle off like the minion I was to catch a train back to my pokey little office.

On said train back to said pokey office, I got a text from a colleague that simply said:

"You're getting sacked in the morning!"

Freaking out and wondering what the hell I'd done I messaged them back, asking if they would at least be kind enough to give me a heads up as to why I would finally be leaving the team.

"Because of your antics in Westminster today," was all I got back.

"And probably because you're such a bellend," he then added for good measure.

Hmmm, apart from taking a selfie in a questionable pose with a statue, for once I'd not done anything to warrant a visit from the HR Hangman.

Five minutes later I settled myself into the routine that every train journey out of London seemed to consist of - checking emails, stuffing my face with crisps, cursing the lack of mobile signal, and trying to avoid falling over thanks to it being standing room only. Amongst the usual emails of "Please receipt this invoice," and "Where is the latest project progress report?" one sent just a few minutes before the earlier text caught my eye. Its title was simply "Busted".

Now, given it was from a dear friend of mine, I was in two minds as to whether she was excitedly emailing me about a reunion of the 2000s pop group or not, and when I opened it I realised no, of course not, she had far better taste than that. What she had emailed out, was in fact a screenshot. A screenshot of the session in Westminster earlier that day.

You see, it turns out the cheeky sods in the office had joined the live stream, and had been looking to see if they could see me and my boss in the room. And it turned out they could.

It also turned out that my nodding and slow blinking routine, combined with the hand on chin pose that I was employing to appear engaged and thoughtful, had created the perfect illusion that I was in actual fact sleeping.

Shit.

It's not a great look to be sat at the back of a room in the powerhouse of this country's government, looking like I'm catching 40 winks and doing it so brazenly next to my own boss...

Credit to her though - the image she'd copied and pasted into the email was perfect. Even I had to think twice as to whether or not I'd actually fallen asleep and somehow developed short-term memory loss and forgotten all about it. And credit to the fact she'd only copied in a handful of colleagues, and not my boss. But the slight problem I had was that we were all very friendly with her manager, who in turn was good friends with my boss, and she'd copied them in. It was only a matter of time before he shared it with my boss and my forays into the upper echelons would end as quickly as they had started.

As they like to say in the good ol' US of A, the aesthetics didn't look good on this one.

In the end my boss did see the email and the incriminating photo. It also turned out he's not such a bad guy after all and wasn't too annoyed at the situation, instead turning it into an excuse for giving me grief and testing me on every single conference call we had for the following two months to check I hadn't fallen asleep without anybody noticing.

The words "Did you get that, Tom?" still bring me out in a cold sweat as my mind leaps into overdrive trying to make sure I can recount what had just been discussed and try to pass the impromptu test.

Well played boss, well played.

And that, ladies and gentlemen, is a subtle way to fuck with someone for supposedly messing up when you give them an opportunity.

I shall definitely be using it as a core tactic in the guerilla warfare that is known as parenting.

Faux pas 22

Eat, drink, work, repeat

As I've mentioned before, like most students I struggled for money whilst at university. Being particularly proud of having grown up saving my own money from weekend jobs to buy myself Playstations, TVs and gifts for my family that were more than just the usual aromatherapy kit for Mum or bottle of whisky for Dad, I wasn't prepared to ask my folks for money to prop me up. It seemed a bit cheeky to say "Hey guys, I know you've saved for countless years to fund my tuition fees and accommodation, but could you bung me some more cash so I can get shitfaced for the umpteenth time this month?"

But enough was enough when I went out for a stroll with my girlfriend towards the end of my first year and we wanted to get a drink and snack from a shop. Not only did I not have any money left in my bank account to pay for anything but I was also £2k into my overdraft - I had maxed it out. Not exactly a great situation to be in. Checking my pockets for change (that was the main method by which people paid for things back in those days, if anyone born after 2003 can believe that) I realised I didn't have enough money for anything resembling a normal drink like a can of Coke, let alone a drink and a snack. All I had was enough to buy a tiny bottle of some god-awful drink called a Panda Pop. We're talking about something absurd like 25p. It doesn't take a genius to figure out that any beverage that costs 25p is not going to be good for you. Hell, even water wouldn't be sold that cheap! It was later on as we shared the last of that tiny bottle of liquified E-numbers and realised dinner was going to be an even bleaker prospect, that I decided I'd need a job for the next year of university.

I was surprised at how hard it was to get a job when I returned to university after the summer - but then again I was a student only available to work evenings and weekends with no experience other than being a fishmonger, so I was probably the only one who was surprised at that.

I probably could've got a job as a bartender, but to be honest I thought another foray into the world of hospitality wasn't a wise idea after my sole day's experience as a waiter. Especially when it would involve being responsible for preparing and serving drinks - my memory is so poor people are genuinely surprised I don't have early on-set dementia, I don't enjoy working under pressure, and I am ridiculously clumsy. To give you a brief insight into my clumsiness I've accidentally poured the boiling water out of a kettle over my hand instead of into the mug, I've knocked drinks over onto legal documents and laptops more times than I care to remember, and I've chopped a fingernail clean off whilst making dinner. So trying to make fifteen Long Island iced teas for a baying mob of female hockey players (the worst animals I've ever witnessed on a night out) when the queue at the bar is three-deep would not end well.

Amazingly I found the perfect job advertised at the local B&Q that ticked all my boxes, and against all expectations I got it. Like I mentioned in a previous chapter it was only stacking shelves in the kitchens and bathrooms department, but I didn't care - there were so many positives to the job that it really was a dream come true. I found myself tidying up the showrooms and keeping the shelves stacked with products, which kept me fit. It was also an evening shift from 8pm until midnight, and so as the shop shut at 9pm I barely had to deal with the public (bar the insomniacs readying themselves for some late night DIY and the lunatics trying to find somewhere half-safe to wander around for an hour or so). This was probably the biggest benefit because on my first shift I was told of the excitement earlier in the day when a customer was being rude to a cashier, and the cashier wasn't having any of it and told them to stop. Not a fan of being challenged, the customer threatened to fight him. Being the City of Portsmouth, steeped in naval history and the fine tradition of brawling that goes with it, the cashier simply said "Come on then," and asked the guy to head outside to the car park. And with that, the cashier took off his garish orange apron, calmly folded it and laid it on the till before walking outside and promptly beating the shit out of the dickhead. Sadly he was sacked, despite his protests that he didn't fight anyone inside the shop. I think what really forced the bosses' hands was the fact it was 3pm on a Saturday and there he was, duking it out in the carpark in front of terrified families before slamming the guy's head into a car so hard it dented it (both the head and the car). Still, what a legend.

Another benefit of the job was there were so few other members of staff on the evening shift that you could easily be in a world of your own, and management was nowhere to be seen thanks to my direct line manager working regular 9-5 hours and being long gone by the time I rocked up.

But it soon dawned on me that it wasn't really the perfect

job, because I'd gotten the job during my second year of university. This was meant to be the best year - the one where you've learned the ropes, got the friends, got your liver used to drinking, don't have to worry about dissertations yet, etc. and yet there I was working 8pm until midnight Monday to Friday whilst my friends were all either out partying or chilling at home getting high and playing FIFA.

Missing out on all that fun was pretty gutting, but I needed the cash... there was no way I was going to struggle for food again so I decided that through being a little bit savvy I could have the best of both worlds. It was a plan destined to fail for sure, but I was desperate to still be part of my friends' plans as much as I could and so my master plan revolved around me heading to the pub with them before I started work. A typical day would see us finish lectures at 4pm and then head to the Student Union bar for a few snakebites (the cause of many a regret on a night out...) before heading home for dinner and then going out again later. Note this was back in the day when people actually went out at a normal time and ended up staggering home at 2am. Not like now where the norm seems to be going out about 11pm and rolling in about 5am. Who the fuck can live a life with those kind of timings? Unless you're a hamster or a vampire that shit is not healthy.

Knowing my friends were happy to drink all day I would persuade them to stay in the pub until about 7pm then I'd rush home, get changed and stumble to work. Diversity was key - thanks to being a social chameleon I had five different circles of friends, and I could persuade each group to stay out after lectures on a different night - for them it was a little bit of pre-drinks ahead of a night out, but for me it was cramming in all of the forthcoming drinking and stupidity into a few hours before I went to work and they went out proper. I have to admit, it didn't take much to convince anyone to drink like that, although it did raise a few eyebrows when I was doing flaming sambucas at 5pm on a Tuesday. One week I wasn't nearly drunk enough to be doing one and as I was launching the glass towards my face I questioned what the hell I was doing. What if it actually burns my throat? Or ignites the rest of the booze in my stomach?! At which point my mind went "Nope!" and at the last minute I tilted my head to the side to avoid it. That was not the smartest move to pull when wanting to bail out of doing a flaming sambuca. Top tip - if you want to abort, just lower the glass. It's far safer. Don't do what I did, because all that will happen is you'll end up hurling lit sambuca down the side of your face, over your ear and sideburn and down the booth you're sitting in - setting fire to all of them. Not being particularly keen to end up looking like Deadpool, that was the last time I lit alcohol before drinking it.

And so a pattern emerged - I would rock up to work pissed, and then spend the following four hours trying to avoid being found out or maimed by some unfortunate accident. Thankfully there were great opportunities to catch a little shuteye - management were keen everyone did training on all manner of things from product knowledge to health and safety, and so I'd waltz up to the training room, settle down at a computer and click a few times through the opening parts of the training modules before promptly falling asleep. With the skeleton crew working evenings and a lone manager covering the whole store, I was never disturbed and could often grab a good hour or two of sleep.

The risk of injury was very real though - whilst occasionally I might drop a tap or a cupboard door, we had some seriously heavy stuff that had to be handled with care and whilst I would've been careful had I known how heavy they were, in my tipsy state I often didn't realise until it was too late. Take for example a Belfast sink. I had no idea these things were as hard to grasp as their namesake accent and just as bone-breaking as the locals. Needing to move one to another shelf I nearly shat out an organ as I suddenly found myself squatting and straining with all my might to stop it from crashing into the ground and smashing into pieces as its true weight became apparent. Who makes a sink that weights 25kg for fuck's sake?! Thankfully I kept my organs out of my pants, although the sink wasn't so lucky. Sorry sink, the combination of my lack of muscles and desire to protect my sphincter meant it was never going to end well for you.

There was also an educational lesson I learned the hard way when I wrote off another item during one of my late-night mishaps. I'd always thought dishwashers and washing machines were pretty much the same thing just with a few tweaks. Pop quiz - who knows that washing machines have a concrete block in the top to stop them thrashing around like they're on speed in a Slipknot mosh pit? Well I didn't, and so you can imagine the surprise I got when I tried to pull one off of a shelf to move it and found myself once again playing the 'will I or won't I shit my pants?' game as I struggled to stop it crashing to the ground. I actually deployed a pretty nifty trick to prevent it from becoming my next victim, although not through any willingness of my own I have to admit - I collapsed under the weight of it and used my body to prevent it from being damaged. Not my smartest move, however, as the tables were turned and it claimed *me* as its next victim - I'm fairly certain I cracked a rib. Then to rub salt in the wound the bloody thing rolled off me and crashed into a metal shelf, cracking the glass and effectively writing it off despite my best efforts to be a human sacrifice and save it from destruction.

A few months into the job and after learning my lesson with the appliances I decided to steer clear of heavy goods and instead focus on becoming more mischievous in my boredom. I probably should've just stopped drinking before work. That would've definitely helped avoid any further faux pas. But alas I was young, dumb and full of rum.

Talking of mischief, the best bit of mischief I've ever heard of was also whilst I was at university. The men's rugby teams embodied mischievousness. Their culture was a dangerous mix of craving laughter, embracing the shock factor and always upping the ante. So it should come as no surprise that one of the teams apparently started playing a game called 'Hide the turd'. No explanation needed for that one I'm sure you'll agree. It was essentially the filthiest game of tag ever played.

In a vase in one lad's lounge, in a trainer, under a sofa… the lads were apparently ticking off a pretty impressive array of locations. I often wonder if they had to take a fresh dump right there, or whether the person who was "it" would have one on their person at all times in a sealed freezer bag, ready to deploy if the perfect opportunity arose. Well anyway, one time nobody had been tagged for ages and people were getting frustrated, wondering if someone had gotten cold feet and quit the game.

And then it happened.

In a masterstroke, the utter deviant whose go it had been clearly decided that they were going to play the long game with their target, and so one morning as one of the lads went to make himself some toast he noticed a strange brown streak in his tub of margarine as he ran the knife across the top. Being bamboozled by this weird mark he scraped at it again. I can only imagine he thought it was some excess Marmite from a previous toast making session. But that's when the smell hit him. Yes, ladies and gentlemen, the last player had lifted the block of margarine out the tub, curled off a length into the tub and then carefully placed the margarine back on top, sealing it in perfectly. God bless the beautiful game of tag and those utterly disgusting degenerates.

I'll be honest, I've set the bar pretty damn high there with that tale, so let's manage expectations - this isn't going to be anywhere near as batshit crazy as that, so settle down.

Back in B&Q, one evening I was hunting for something in the warehouse and decided I'd check if my manager had put it in his office, so peering through the window I spotted what I was looking for and tried the door handle. It was unlocked. Bingo. I ventured in.

The office had all the hallmarks of a man who didn't really care about much - crisp wrappers littered the floor, a photo of his kids was wedged behind a pile of brochures, his coffee mug looked like he was trying to grow some new strain of super bacteria, and his chair looked like it had been upholstered with a tramp's clothes. Hideous. But, there above the filing cabinets behind his desk was a pristine team poster of his beloved Portsmouth F.C. On top of the filing cabinets were trinkets, framed match day programmes, and all kinds of Portsmouth F.C. memorabilia. It was all pristine and not a hint of a crisp wrapper was anywhere in sight. Holy shit, I thought, it was his shrine.

Two things crossed my mind. One, I didn't like the team very much after they'd beaten my beloved team a few weeks earlier. Two, I wondered how much he'd lose his shit if someone messed with it. Combined together, you know where this was going. Armed with a permanent marker, I set about that poster less like Michelangelo painting the Sistine Chapel and more like a third-rate Banksy tagging the wall of an underpass. I'm not going to lie, I revelled in that moment. The excitement was palpable - to be caught defacing the manager's property would no doubt be a sackable offence, but I was riding the heady mix of adrenaline combined with five pints of Fosters and three tequilas.

After the obligatory top hats, moustaches, devil tails and of course, penises, were added to his precious team photo I carefully exited the office making sure nobody saw me, and slipped back into the warehouse like nothing had happened - but with a hell of a smile on my face. I've been told on several occasions that I look like a smug twat so I can only imagine what I looked like as I waltzed around the shop that night, proud as punch with my efforts.

The next day I went in for my usual shift expecting all hell to have broken loose. But alas nothing had happened. I couldn't exactly ask people if he'd noticed the graffiti on his beloved poster, so I resigned myself to the fact I'd just have to wait until he noticed.

Well, clearly the bloody poster was also one of the things he didn't care about as he didn't notice for weeks. It made no sense as it was his shrine. Maybe he was going through a divorce and was severely distracted. From my perspective, as someone with OCD who freaks out when a picture frame is wonky (both because it disrupts the angles and lines of a room and because I worry I'm being spied on) that must surely have been the only reason it took so long for him to register it. The good news is it was worth the wait - word spread through the day crews and into the night crews that he had lost his mind, claiming he'd chop the fingers off whoever had done it. Ah, Portsmouth - it truly is the city of unrestrained savages.

Realising he'd never see the funny side of it, I kept quiet, not even telling my colleagues on the night shift who normally enjoyed giving the day crew a bit of grief. Then one day my manager was having to work late after a busy day.

"Tom, are you alright to finish packing these damaged returns up and putting them back in the warehouse for disposal tomorrow?" he asked, exhaling a long sigh as he loaded another broken cupboard door onto the trolley.

"Of course, no problem at all."

"Ah," he muttered, "I don't know where my pen's gone. I need to mark these up with the right details. Can I quickly borrow one?"

"Sure," I said, passing him a pen from the stash I kept in

my work apron.

The look on his face. I won't forget it. His tired but friendly expression dropped, like he was having an emotional stroke. Soon it was replaced with an icy glare. Which is funny because it felt like it was burning a hole in me. It was every bit the expression you see in movies where the undercover cop gets rumbled and the mafia boss who's taken them under their wing looks at them with pure hatred. Turns out, yes I'd crept out of his office after defacing his poster without anyone noticing, but crucially I'd forgotten to put back his permanent marker, instead keeping it as my own. Cat thief of the year I'm sure you'll agree. Realising I'd just handed it back to him, I looked down to the ground, blinked slowly, took a breath and did the most comedy of gulps like every bad guy does in the cartoons when they're clearly in the shit.

Subconsciously remembering his finger-chopping threat, I found myself clenching mine tightly as I awaited my fate. But he said nothing. At least not verbally. His unrelenting eye contact, frown and body language, however, said *I'm going to fuck you up*.

Credit to him though, he never laid a finger on me (or any of mine for that matter). He was actually quite savvy, and instead messed with me in quite understated ways. The one that worked best was the security checks. At the end of every shift staff would have to line up by the exit and take part in the shittest form of lottery ever. It involved taking turns to step forward to a black box with a hole cut in the top, reach in and pick out a ball. You see there were several balls inside, but one was a special ball - if you picked that one, you and any bag you might have with you was searched. Turns out folk love to steal. And folks working for a DIY store apparently have such sticky fingers that they border on being kleptomaniacs. Rumour had it that one guy at our store used to steal really expensive drill bits, and resorted to sticking them up his arse before the end of his shift to avoid being caught. So if you buy second hand nearly new drill bits in Portsmouth, my advice is to give them a really good wash first.

Anyway, I had only drawn the security check ball once in the four months I'd been working there up to the point of being rumbled as the wannabe Banksy. But from then on, I drew it nearly every shift. It was unbearable. After being stuck there for four hours doing my shift when the clock finally struck midnight I just wanted to get home and crash out, ready to start my lectures at 9am the next day (my course was a real fucker often with days full of lectures from 9am to 4pm, unlike my housemates' courses which only asked them to turn up to four lectures a week). The last thing I needed was to get stuck there being searched and quizzed by security.

At first I thought it was pure coincidence, but then I realised that couldn't be possible and instead the security guard manning that little black box was deploying some Derren Brown sleight of hand shit to keep landing me with the dreaded security check ball. I was starting to lose my shit, and could do nothing but applaud my manager's ingenuity at implementing this scheme.

After three more weeks of 'winning' the security lottery at virtually every shift I caved in, lost my shit during the search and quit on the spot. Then I had to quit again the next day because my manager wasn't there to witness it, which kind of took the edge off the gesture for me, but for him it ensured he was able to observe the end to his game of chess and bathe in the glory of forcing me out. I think that's called closure.

Bravo boss, I learned a lot that day - you've helped instil in me a belief that if I'm devious and cunning enough, I can get any result I want. And if I'm really good at it, I can fuck someone up in the process.

So there's a little warning to my kids - you best stop waking me up in the middle of the night and screaming in the car, because one day you're going to expect some inheritance and BOOM - my lawyers will inform you I've blown it all and actually left you with some debts like the round the world cruise you thought my pension was paying for. Wise up, motherfuckers!

Faux pas 23

Polos - the ~~mint~~ hedge with the hole

In the period of my career when I was still in sales, I was driving in to the office one wintery day when something terrifying but awesome happened. Whilst attempting to park my little VW Polo it turned out that the smattering of snow on the ground was actually a lot more slippery than I gave it credit for, and so instead of simply pulling into the space I ended up spinning uncontrollably... but after doing a full 360° spin I somehow ended up smack bang in the middle of a parking space! Admittedly it wasn't the one I was aiming for, but hey, that's a minor detail. The main thing is I performed a move like I was a seasoned Hollywood stunt performer and every cell in my body felt alive for the first time in years.

The next day the snow still hadn't cleared, and so wanting to experience the thrill once more I decided to try and repeat the feat.

Knowing that the snow was the secret ingredient to carrying out the stuntman-esque car slide into the parking space, I should have simply repeated every single action from the day before and success would have been assured, as a) the ground was still covered in snow, b) I was still driving my beloved Polo, and c) I had absolutely no technique when it came to performing driving tricks. By no technique I mean no idea. And by tricks I mean even the simplest of things other than going forwards or backwards. I couldn't even do a wheelspin, bar the one time where I was wearing a brand new pair of brogues and ended up accidentally mashing multiple pedals whilst pulling away from some traffic lights. I have to admit though, I lost all credibility thanks to my high-pitched squealing as I unexpectedly took off at Mach 3.

But alas, merely repeating the same routine as yesterday would've been far too easy. Copying yesterday's moves felt like cheating - at the end of the day, whether it's copying someone else's homework or your own series of movements, plagiarism is plagiarism, and the hollow feeling that haunts any subsequent success means it's never worth it. Oh no, I needed the hit of pure unbridled ingenuity once again, and so, feeling like the spirit of Colin McRae was alive within me, I drove at speed towards the business park.

Careering into the entrance I quickly slowed down, showing the other office workers bumbling through the car park that I knew my shit, that I knew how to handle a beast in all weather, like a Formula 1 driver entering the pit lanes at 50mph after hurtling around a track at over 200 mph. I caught a glimpse of myself in the rearview mirror and afforded myself a wry smile - I even looked the part with my Aviator sunglasses. Shame I was driving a Polo. Not only that, it had faded into a shade of pink thanks to a terrible paint job in the late nineties. It definitely killed the look I was going for.

Nearing our company's section of the car park I decided to really give it some oomph, aiming to better yesterday's good feat with something truly monumental today. As I said, I had absolutely zero idea what the fuck I should be doing with the pedals and handbrake, but having watched pretty much every action movie of the past decade that featured impeccable handbrake turns and power slides, I convinced myself that I had grasped the basics. And so with that I went into beast mode, channeling my inner stunt man. In lieu of any actual knowledge I instead aimed to rely purely on gut-instinct, which was instantly a red flag for guaranteed disaster, because whilst I'd previously managed to succeed with trusting my gut, I've got to admit that was with some pretty basic tasks like how hard to hit a ball in snooker or how much to push out a fart without following through. This, however, was a one ton block of metal on ice. And there was always that incident at the bar in Portsmouth which showed my gut wasn't always to be trusted… I'll leave you to guess whether it was missing a shot in snooker or shitting my pants.

And so I stomped on the pedals in fast-paced alternating fashion like the lovechild of Michael Flatley and Lewis Hamilton, spun the steering wheel and yanked on the handbrake, hoping like a kid playing Street Fighter back in the 90s that the *press all the buttons really fast in a random order* move would result in a mind-blowing victory. Interestingly the car moved a lot faster than the day before, and rather than spinning around and coming to a nice stop a few spaces into the company's parking area, it decided a 45 degree turn was all it was going to muster and instead sent me careering towards the nice leafy car park divider. Turns out, snow freezes, and I was not driving on nice powdery snow like the day before, aka the wet dream of snowboarders and skiers. Oh no, I was driving on sheet ice, the kind even Eskimos and polar bears look at and think "Nah, fuck that."

They say time slows down when you're in stressful situations like a car crash or a gunfight. Clearly this didn't meet the bar set for a bonafide car crash, because time did not slow down one iota. I barely had enough time to squeal "Fuck!" before physics helped the hedge and my car reach their natural conclusion.

It was at the point where the bonnet and a good portion of windscreen were already inside the 10ft high hedge that I began to realise that Hollywood had once again lied to me, luring me into a false sense of confidence about how to really nail a handbrake turn. There's actually a long and embarrassing list of things I've developed flawed logic for thanks to using the medium of movies as my Life Coach: how to drink; how to have banter with strangers; how to fight; how to chat up women; how to look good naked; how to handle rejection… And so in line with all of those life failures, this was not the triumph of driving skill I had anticipated, oh no, this was simply another lesson in humility.

I honestly believe if you want to get an insight into someone's psyche (i.e. the basic principles that they hold dear, and what their reactions are to stress, humiliation and anguish) then don't bother with weeks of tedious and expensive therapy sessions - just get them to crash their car into a hedge outside their office whilst trying to show off, and see how they extricate not only their car from said hedge, but themselves from the awkward social situation they then find themselves in. It's hard to hide one's true feelings when your colleagues might be watching, you're facing a week of eating beans for dinner because you've got to pay for the repairs to your car, and when you have to own up to the fact you're just not as good a driver as you thought you were.

For me, it was the shame that was going to be the hardest knock to take. I was already earning peanuts (which ironically prevented me from eating them - have you seen the price of a bag of salted cashews?! Daylight fucking robbery) and so was used to one unforeseen outlay a month rendering me a peasant for the remainder of it until payday. I was also under no illusion that I was a good driver - like a WW2 fighter pilot, my beloved Polo had the etchings of confirmed skirmishes on its bodywork which it wore with pride: six kerbs, one hatchback, a fence and a pheasant (which I can only presume was wearing a crash helmet given the damage it caused my bumper).

Putting it into reverse and gingerly backing out of what was left of the bastard hedge, I sighed as I prepared myself for the torrent of abuse about to be launched my way from the rest of the company who were carefully parking their cars like grown ups in the snowy car park. But alas, whilst the timing of my manoeuvres was truly horrendous, the timing of the overall debacle was perfect - I'd hit a sweet spot of pulling in at 08:58. This was the no man's land in between the organised colleagues who ensured they arrived early enough to start work bang on 9am, and the colleagues who were clearly thinking "fuck you" as they religiously turned up at 09:05. And so I afforded myself a smug little smile as I delicately steered my shit-heap of a car into the parking space I'd originally aimed for, and relaxed. I'd done it. I'd fucked up, made a right tit of myself, and damaged company property - but I'd gotten away with it. Boom. It was time to crack out a bit of swagger on the walk over to the office.

But mid-way through my strutting I looked up to the first floor of the office and I stopped a damn sight quicker than my Polo had as I saw the FD stood in his office window, mouth open, aghast at what he'd just witnessed.

Fuck.

I had a fairly good rapport with our FD, so was hoping he'd be fairly ambivalent towards the clear breaking of a fair few company rules and the obliteration of a hedge. As I looked up at him and gulped, I watched as he mouthed the words "What a twat," before shaking his head and walking away. Possibly to tell the MD and help draft up my P45, possibly to just make himself another coffee. The jury was out.

Fuck it.

I really needed this job. I mean REALLY needed it - I'd already been through the wringer to get it and now needed it more than ever. You see, when I started dating my wife, she put an expiry date on us unless I learned to drive (yeah, she's like that). She also gave me an ultimatum of us needing to live together as she couldn't be arsed with the long distance dating thing. I'm sure she put it in nicer words than that, but maybe not - she's blessed with the gift of brutality that comes from having both a totalitarian father and IT sales experience. So I was forced (sorry, *encouraged*) to get a job closer to where she lived, and back then the only offer I had remaining after the disastrous interview at the Atomic Weapons Establishment was for a sales role. Thinking it would be a simple interview for a specific role, I was in fact greeted with some batshit crazy day that was like a cross between The Apprentice and The Hunger Games.

Let me enlighten you. Walking into the building on the outskirts of West London I was taken to a room where about thirty desperate job hunters were corralled into the middle, whilst the interviewers and prospective employers sat around the perimeter of the room like voyeurs enjoying some kind of illegal or primitive sport like cockfighting or rugby league. They explained to us that the day was going to involve a series of challenges, and whilst we'd be split into teams we would be monitored for signs of tact, strategy, teamplay and decisiveness, with the employers and interviewers all keenly observing and taking notes. There was such a focus on observing how we acted that I was genuinely surprised when I wasn't followed into the toilet by someone with a notepad.

But before it all got started, we'd been told that this was essentially like playing sports at school, where at the end the employers would pick who they wanted until the group was whittled down to those who they simply didn't, and therefore were destined to join the growing numbers of unemployed but eager to work folk (this was right after the 2008 financial crash). I was acutely aware of this, and the fact that I had my whole future with my then-girlfriend hinging on me landing a job from the Hunger Games day left me shaking like a shitting dog. I was also sweating profusely. I'll never forget the lead interviewer greeting me and seeing them grimace as they felt my sweaty palm squelch against theirs as we shook hands. She actually asked me "Do you have a condition?" I'm not exactly sure what condition would result in sweating excessively from the palms, but I contemplated telling her I did. In the end I simply mumbled "Er, no…" and literally hung my head in shame, staring at the floor like an embarrassed schoolboy.

Knowing this was make or break time I went full tilt, conveying my best Wolf of Wall Street persona to see this over the line and leave every employer present in no doubt that I needed to be hired. It didn't exactly get off to the best start, however, with an exercise that saw us split into two teams and aiming to complete a matrix of information. Seeing my chance to shine, I went over my team captain's head and struck up a friendship with someone from the opposite team, and proceeded to steal all their info whilst simultaneously feeding them lies in return, screwing them over and setting us up for the win. I was feeling pretty smug as we walked back into the main room when the exercise ended, but that emotion was replaced pretty quickly with shame once again as I was singled out in front of the entire room for my underhand and devious tactics, with the unwritten but intended rules for the day apparently being team spirit and mutually beneficial deals over sniping and underhand tactics.

After that, I decided to be less Wolf of Wall Street and more me, and the rest of the day actually ended up going pretty well.

But at the end of it, during the humiliating culling of interviewees, I found myself being one of the unfortunate few who were left without a hiring company - my apparent lack of a direct sales attitude being the main reason. I couldn't bloody win! Feeling distraught and wondering what horrible jobs I'd have to consider in order to secure employment and the ability to move in with my girlfriend (and really hoping it wouldn't be another attempt at the used underwear sales from my university days), I was surprised to be asked to stay behind along with another interviewee. As the room cleared out we were joined by the Head of the team who was leading the recruitment day. It turned out that whilst no employers wanted us, the recruitment company felt that we had the personal skills and friendly nature that would fit right into their setup and so we were offered jobs there and then to join them! Neither of us could believe it.

I was on cloud nine, and went back a week later to get down to the nitty gritty of discussing salaries and bonus structure. I even went for after-work beers with the team as we were all certain I'd be joining them in a few weeks. But then something weird happened. During beers and talks with my future manager, she asked what my situation was at home. I mentioned the plans to use the job to be able to finally move in with my girlfriend to avoid being ditched, and how we were planning to live just outside the M25 so we'd both be within commuting distance of our respective jobs. I immediately saw a sneer appear on her face. I cocked my head quizzically. Seeing my little boy lost expression, she chipped in with "You won't last long. Don't bother getting a place together…"

"Sorry, what?" I replied, my head now tilting the other way to make sure I heard her correctly.

"Every single person who started with us and had a partner didn't stay with them longer than six months. It's just how it is. We are a team that works long hours and we enjoy socialising as a team too, and that often leaves little time for partners at home. It's just how it is."

"Riiiiiight," I said slowly, still trying to come to terms with what this was. To help, she cleared it up quite nicely for me.

"We're a young and attractive team, and most of us end up dating each other as we know what the score is. There's a lot of fun to be had. Lizzy's already told me she likes you, and I saw you looking at Erica earlier... You'll be fine once you join, just don't rent anywhere outside London as I won't employ anyone who isn't able to get on the Tube - it just doesn't work and I can't be bothered wasting my time if someone is going to jack it in a few months down the line because of the commute."

I have to admit I did start to wonder what a debauched lifestyle in sales in London would be like - a friend who worked for a large estate agent in London would frequently regale us with tales down the pub about parties with bathtubs full of booze, getting blowjobs from assistants, and some seriously freaky stuff with one night stands. It was pure and utter hedonism. But then I remembered I wasn't Hugh Heffner and had an incredible girlfriend back home (I was punching so far above my weight that I'm pretty sure one time someone thought she was my carer) and that a life with her was worth far more than a couple of crazy, filthy, wild parties and series of one night stands. Many years of marriage later, and I don't think I'd be quite so honourable, but hey I was young and naive!

And so I had to politely push back on the suggestions of ditching the Mrs and living within the M25. Oh how she turned. It was instant. I can even remember the moment her face stopped smiling and it became apparent that I was merely an outsider, a stranger who was interrupting their work drinks and was no longer welcome in their space. Shrugging, I finished my pint and walked out, called my estate agent friend and went to meet him to discuss what had just happened. Namely what I was going to do with no sign of employment on the horizon, having gambled it all to stay honest for the girl I loved, despite the fact that if the gamble didn't pay off I'd lose her.

He was mortified that I had turned down the chance to join him in Sin City and paint the town red every night. And he didn't mince his words. That was his style. I once told him I was dating an on/off-again ex-girlfriend for the eighth time after a series of brutal breakups and incidents over the years. His response? To stop being all smiley and full of banter, and stare me right in the eyes and say "Do not go out with her again. If you do, I will strangle you." It was such a surreal and personal threat of dispatching me delivered with such sincerity that I heeded his advice, and broke it off with her as quickly as it had restarted. Turns out it was pretty sage advice - she later converted to Islam, and given her temper and the inability to predict what she might do when angry I really wouldn't have wanted MI5 keeping tabs on our every move. Or worse yet, monitoring my internet browsing habits. Lord no - I watched some pretty devious filth whilst at university, to the point where when I graduated I destroyed my computer's hard drive with a combination of a hammer, an industrial magnet (yes those fucking things stayed with me even after splitting the end of my nose) and fire. So much fire.

Thankfully only a few weeks later the company said they'd passed on my CV to an IT sales company and they were keen to bring me in for an interview.

I researched the hell out of the sector, the company and their products, and smashed the interview - so much so that I got offered the job by the time I'd driven back to my girlfriend's parents' house! After the congratulatory hugs and kisses she was straight onto rightmove.co.uk looking for places to live, and within a few weeks we were renting a flat together. One year later whilst walking through the neighbourhood we could see all these couples and families in their lovely houses and made the decision to get on the property ladder. That moment was the week before I stuck my Polo into the hedge in full view of the FD, triggering my panic about being fired as no job obviously means no ability to get a mortgage.

Back at the carpark, having watched the FD call me a twat and waltz off into the main area of the office, I was shitting my pants as I made my way towards the entrance.

Gingerly stepping into the lobby I paused to try and listen to what conversations were taking place, and see if I was walking into an ambush or whether the coast was clear. I could hear him in the kitchen - he was making a coffee after all and not grassing me up to the MD! Stepping into the kitchen, we locked eyes as if we were two cowboys about to have a duel, our only exchange a simple greeting.

"Jim."

"Tom."

The tension was annoying me, I needed to find out what his plan was, because whilst sticking your car in a hedge is fairly minor in the list of offences at a company, the MD was strict and the CEO was even stricter (he was downright terrifying). Mind you, there was some hope as another young colleague had been caught *feeding the pony* with the receptionist in the toilets at a Christmas party the year before and kept his job. Although to be fair he was one of the top performing salesmen and my only success had actually caused more problems than it had been worth thanks to it involving a Russian oligarch... Thanks to the NDA I signed and their nation's penchant for poisoning people, that's all I'm going to say about that!

Sensing my nerves, Jim put me out of my misery pretty quickly.

"Don't worry about what happened in the car park," he reassured me, "we all thought you were a crap driver and this just confirmed our suspicions."

Phew - thank fuck for that. To be fair, Jim was a pretty decent guy, and it should've come as no surprise he was cool with it, as he had top notch banter and had no qualms about breaking the unwritten rules of how Directors engage with regular employees. I still remember an incident where I couldn't figure out how to load some official headed paper into the printer to print off some documents needed for the financial element of a deal. There's only so many combinations of ways round or up that you can try before you get it right, but for some reason I just couldn't figure it out and kept printing the info on the back of the paper or upside down. Seeing me nipping back and forth between my computer and the printer, and getting angrier each time, Jim wandered over.

"What you trying to do, Tom?" he asked.

"I can't figure out how this fucking headed paper needs to be loaded into the tray to print off the bank details for this deal we're pushing through," I replied, exasperated.

"Oh right, I see. Well the thing to remember is it's just how your Mum likes it - face down, arse first."

What. The. Actual. Fuck.

And with that, we were both in hysterics. See, providing they're not dead, you can't go wrong with a good Mum joke!

Faux pas 24

Never get caught

Long before I was duly sacked from the job selling to construction companies (for dropping the c-bomb so loud it inadvertently featured in every other call taking place in the office) I had lost the respect of every single one of my colleagues.

For me that's nothing new. But this particular time definitely made me cringe, and still does to this day.

There are certain things you shouldn't get caught doing at work. I'm not talking the kind of shit that would get you featured on Crimewatch, more the kind of stuff where people question your character, how much they should talk to you in future, and whether they'll be gossiping about you with their friends or not when conversation turns to weirdos we've met lately.

And it's this kind of incident that resulted in most of them not liking my character, talking to me a lot less afterwards, and 100% telling all their friends that I was the grubby little weirdo in their office.

As I mentioned in the earlier chapter recalling my faux pas of dropping the c-bomb, about 95% of the staff were women. With this came a certain level of expectation - be polite, maintain a basic level of hygiene, bitch but don't bully, and don't be disgusting.

I was, and always will be, keen to make sure I could

seamlessly slip into the clique and be accepted as one of the girls (they never judge how camp I am) so I reined the potty mouth in, made sure I washed my hands after taking a pee, threw some light-hearted sass about and avoided burping or farting anywhere in the vicinity of the office.

One particular day, however, I was struggling to contain some particularly aromatic 'bum burps' after another poorly judged combination the night before of red meat and several pints of ale. Once that medley lands in my stomach I'm fairly certain my entire body starts counting down to a point the next day when it decides to press the big red button and launch the nukes. I'd done really well for much of the day, not even attempting to deep-bed anything into a chair and instead headed into the men's toilet each time to let rip.

Interestingly my colleagues would all go outside for a cigarette break every couple of hours, even though not all of them smoked. The lure of having a good gossip was clearly too much to resist for some. By late afternoon they were all on their third cigarette break, and I found myself sat in the deserted office. Knowing they wouldn't be back for another 10-15 minutes I realised I could be the absolute degenerate that I was for at least five blissful minutes. I wasn't exactly going around shitting on desks, but I was enjoying not having to maintain the expectations for a short while. It can be surprisingly hard work when you've spent so long around guys who take great pride in burping, farting and generally being as rude, crude and disgusting as possible all in the name of comedy.

I decided to afford myself the simple pleasure of staying seated whilst releasing a ripper of a fart. No walk downstairs to the men's toilet for that one. Oh no, I sat there and let rip, even giving it a bit of extra oomph to really embrace the moment. I know, I'm a filthy boy who should behave better, but this is real life and we all do it. I'd just like to point out that some of the worst/best burps and farts have come from women I know! My wife once let out an absolute corker in a restaurant whilst laughing at one of my jokes on our first date, and that will live long in my memory - along with my rare display of selflessness as I loudly apologised to spare her the embarrassment.

Deciding to really embrace a bit of carpe diem I thought why not truly enjoy the moment and check out the effort? They say everyone likes their own brand. I have to admit I never savoured the smell of my bum burps, but there was some kind of morbid curiosity to checking out what they were like. A lot like when you tread in dog shit, you know it's going to smell awful but you just can't help but take a whiff. And more often than not, wretch immediately after.

Looking around just to make absolutely sure there was nobody else in the office, I leant down and inhaled. Now I'm not really sure whether it was because I couldn't smell anything or because I really wanted to get a full appreciation of it, but I found myself using my hand to waft the aroma towards my face.

Quite disgraceful I'm sure you'll agree. It's disgraceful anywhere. In the privacy of your home would still be bad enough, but in the office - that's downright dirtbag behaviour. There's still a leap between disgraceful and mortifying, though. It takes that unique element of witnesses and the subsequent shame to really round it off and morph disgraceful into mortifying.

And that leads us nicely to what happened next - you see, whilst the ladies would have happily stayed outside for nearly 15 minutes and let me get away with my dirty deed, mother nature had other ideas. Yes that's right, it started to rain. And with that, they came streaming into the office, silent though for some reason, like a bunch of perfumed ninjas. And they walked straight in to see me sat there, bent over, wafting my fart into my face and taking a big old sniff.

Mortifying.

My true colours had been bared for all to see, and the ladies had in that moment learned what I truly was - an utter filthbag who hadn't evolved from being a dirty teenager. Their faces were a picture. It's really hard to forget a face when it contorts so much to cover all the key bases of disgust, pity and loathing. And so there was a weird kind of Mexican stand-off - they kept standing and staring and I kept looking up at them from my bent over position with a look of pure helplessness. People say about wanting the ground to open up and swallow them, but until this happened I didn't really appreciate how true that phrase is - I yearned for it to happen. *Yearned* for it.

I can't remember what broke the deadlock, but I do remember the murmuring and tutting as they wandered back to their desks, clearly starting the distancing from me (social and physical) and vowing to tell everyone who would listen what a fart-sniffing weirdo I was.

So the moral of the story? Never get caught. If you want to be a dirtbag then go right ahead. Just do it in the comfort of your own home, or at least a cubicle if you're such a deviant that you can't refrain whilst at work.

Faux pas 25

Conference conflict

Early on in my time at the engineering firm I was lucky enough to work on an impressive project which generated lots of interest across a number of industries. I've got to admit though, I didn't exactly jump at the opportunity - I only found out I had the role when the Head of our department was chairing the kick-off meeting for it and put a slide up with my name next to this particular position.

I think he clocked me starting to mouth "What the fu..." and said "Oh, have you not been notified yet? Okay, well, here it is - congratulations on your new role!" And so like so many other times throughout my career, I found myself being the last to know and also the focus of the laughter in the room. But truth be told I didn't care if people were laughing with me or at me - laughter just has a glorious effect on me, like someone turning up the contrast and colour settings on a TV and making everything brighter, warmer and just that little bit more enjoyable. It's like a drug, and I'm a junkie that craves it. The trouble is, that craving tends to overrule the part of my brain which is trying to temper the court jester approach, often doing so when the situation really calls for the utmost professionalism.

The role itself was great, namely because a group of contractors were delivering the bulk of the project so I just had to make sure things were sticking to the rules and timescales, and be the spokesperson for our company when we were asked to discuss it in a meeting or at a conference. I didn't have much to worry about as they were a great team, and as we were all keeping things going so smoothly it meant when in spokesperson mode I was able to be pretty confident, gung-ho and if I'm completely honest, smug. By now you know the routine - it wasn't going to end well...

Within only a short period of time there was a lot of positivity around the project and our company's stock was rising off the back of it (sadly not literally though), so we were invited to present at a conference which was showcasing the best projects our industry had to offer. Given the event was going to be attended by governments, investors and other people who could easily mess with your future, you can imagine how surprised I was when the powers that be suggested I be the one who goes up on stage and presents.

I had officially been offered as a sacrifice to the conference gods.

Incredibly, the presentation itself went without a hitch - which was probably down to the contractors actually doing the bulk of it, like one of those duets where one person spends 90% of the song just nodding with their eyes closed, savouring the fact the other singer is doing all the hard graft and occasionally chipping in with a few words here and there. Once done we settled down to be part of 'the panel' where despite all the glitz and glamour of the venue, the conference's production values had dropped significantly and we were presented with a hastily assembled medley of chairs, a table not big enough to allow all the presenters to sit around it, and a table cloth which I later learned didn't reach the floor. This meant everyone could see my neon yellow The Simpsons socks and immediately get the measure of me as the immature smart arse that I was.

Trying to avoid revelling in the fact that I'd managed to get an actual seat at the table (unlike poor Jason from a big conglomerate who would no doubt be mocked by his workmates for being part of the panel but ending up stuck on a chair nowhere near the table) I was surprisingly overcome by nerves. What was going on? What could have triggered such a thing to happen? I had no problems posing for a photo with only a clump of seaweed protecting my modesty whilst completely sober on a university field trip years earlier, so what the hell was this all about? Needing to get a grip, I channelled my inner daytime TV host and tried to put on my best *I'll smile even if you make this an absolute car crash of an interview* look.

It was working. I was able to respond to the questions thrown at me from the audience with aplomb, even gaining enough confidence to chip in on one or two other panel members' responses. Recognising that I was running the risk of getting carried away, I decided to rein it in and simply sit there, smile the confident smile I'd put on the whole time I was on the panel, and hope to make it to the end of the session without any curveball questions that would highlight my thin veneer of knowledge. Simple.

It's always the last question, though, isn't it?

Step right on up, Annabelle. Opening with the fact her question was for me, she disarmed me with her smile and friendly tone. I was expecting something like "So what's next for this golden-goose project? Make it even bigger and better? Roll it out across the country?" Instead it was a completely unnecessary, tricky and downright shitty question about the rights of customers, insinuating we were taking liberties. Well fuck me, she was a bonafide wolf in sheeps' clothing - the devil masquerading as a civil servant. That might seem a tad strong, but she was aiming to take me down in front of a room full of people on my conference panel debut. Not cool.

Falling back on a combination of my years of quick-fire banter with friends and dealing with the scathing abuse a former Scottish colleague liked to level at me, I quickly pivoted my stance and went on the attack - shooting her down by not only answering the question but also highlighting that it was in fact a ridiculous one.

Oh it felt good. I mean sure I'd gambled, but I'd won big, and I was able to let the tension drift away from my hunched shoulders and enjoy my first time on stage once more, stretching my legs out and unwittingly giving everyone an even better glimpse of Homer Simpson.

Cue my return to TV host *smiling and powering on through* mode with a few added extras thrown in for good measure, like a nod of the head here and a pensive expression there. You know, to give that added air of "I know my shit, I deserve to be at the table." And then finally it was over. Thank god for that, I thought. I soaked up the applause, absurdly losing myself in the moment and starting to bow, like some absolute bellend thinking he's on stage in a West End production. That forced me to then pretend I was in fact bending down to get closer to the table to carefully scrutinise my notes, which would have looked plausible to the attendees but like utter madness to my fellow panellists as it was clear for all to see that there was in fact nothing on the table in front of me.

And with that I was free!

I found myself almost, yes almost, skipping back to our stand to regale my colleagues with the tale of how I'd faced adversity head-on and beaten the beast, like some kind of medieval warrior returning from battle full of bravado. It's incredible the psychological boost you get from a little win like that - not since I clocked that wanker Dave Gibson in the face with a conker when I was 10 years old had I felt such elation, such power.

Of course nobody gave a shit, and soon it was the end of the conference and the magic words of "Free drinks anyone?" were muttered. Ah yes, free booze… the readily dispensed alcohol acting as the social lubricant needed to help you glide effortlessly between talks of families and workplace woes and the desperate attempts to sell new products and services. I never did understand either of those - why, when faced with a chance to kick back and let loose and have fun would you treat it like a bit of free counselling? And equally if you've not managed to persuade someone to buy something in the preceding eight hours, give up the ghost, it ain't happening - just have another bottle of lukewarm beer and stop working.

The drinks are normally laid on by a rather nice sponsor, which definitely blurs the lines between work and social time and so you always end up with a beautiful kaleidoscope of characters turning up to sample the beverages. Without fail each and every one of these complimentary drinks receptions over the years ended up with the same characters rocking up, all with varying temperaments, tolerances and dispositions, which were then magnified thanks to the wonders of free drink.

I've no doubt these characters will have been witnessed at any conference throughout the history of time where the fatal words "Free drinks?!" are whispered with excitement.

Let's begin the roll call:

The wallflower - these folks are terrified of social interactions, epitomising the definition of a wallflower by skirting the fringes of the room and only venturing into the inner circle of activity to get a drink (which is likely to be a soft one). They won't even make their excuses to leave, instead discretely slipping away and scurrying back to the safety of their hotel room and the joys of solo dining thanks to the wonders of room service.

The peacock - buoyed by a successful day of sales/networking/presenting, they strut around with a smugness reserved for criminals who've escaped a jail sentence for a crime they definitely committed, oozing confidence and possibly a bit too much aftershave. They draw an equal array of admiration and resentment from the room.

The jester - their confidence knows no bounds. For me this is triggered when I'm exactly one and a half glasses of rosé wine in. At times the banter is relentless, bordering on the inappropriate and occasionally they do like to become loud and very animated with their comedy, causing some people to distance themselves as it all ramps up a notch.

The teetotaller - they don't drink, which is fine, but equally they don't seem to have social skills either, so just make things awkward for everyone. They soon become very judgy as others slip into the warm haze of inebriation, like some kind of militant vegan at any kind of social gathering involving food.

The observer - these folks just like to stand quietly watching the comings and goings, noting who does or says what. They are the equivalent of a photo gallery on your phone, because the next day they will be the reliable source of truth, unlike everyone else's alcohol-addled memories.

The worm - these people just appear, silently, next to your group, looking to work their way into a conversation. You feel sorry for them and look to welcome them, but soon get annoyed at their lack of input and so they will eventually be cut from the group and left to worm their way into another conversation.

The bulldozer - they take no prisoners with their tactics of steaming into groups, smashing conversations and social norms to pieces and forcing themselves and their very vocal thoughts into other people's evenings. Drawing more judging looks and tuts than a queue jumper, their time within each group is limited, but they couldn't care less.

The alcoholic - collecting drinks like a kleptomaniac, they will be in awe at the ability to consume as many drinks as they want when they want without paying, which unsurprisingly leads to the swaying, slurred words and droopy eyelids that signal the rapidly approaching end of their night (despite the fact it may well only be 7:30pm).

Which one are you? Come on, you know which one you turn into the minute you're away from the office, away from home and free from the shackles of your boss, your other half and the bastard kids - or maybe, like me, you are a chameleon of post-conference drinks receptions and find yourself transforming into each character at some stage in the night... For me, it starts out with a brief stint as the observer before a rapid growth in confidence sees me rise through the peacock phase until I explode in a crescendo of noise and energy as the jester of the scene, closely followed by the bulldozer and alcoholic until the drink completely takes over and then I'm on the other side, being consumed by self-doubt and intoxicated anxiety and my descent begins. I will then find myself steadily falling into the worm mentality, then free falling into wallflower territory before finally crash landing into being the teetotaller - not through choice but because I've inevitably been refused any more alcohol by the concerned bar staff. I feel it necessary to point out my plight as a lightweight means this entire character arc takes place over the course of a mere four glasses of wine, rosé if they have it thank you very much. On a side note, never ask for a glass of rosé wine at a pub in Glasgow. I found this out the hard way. If you're of the fairer sex you might get away with it, but if you're a posh Englishman you might end up with an experience like mine - being eyed with much disgust before someone threatens to punch you in the face for asking for such a despicable drink, whilst another helpfully points out "We don't sell cocktails in here, sweetheart."

I have no doubt there's some deep-rooted psychological issues at play with my drinking, and one day it'll probably all come flooding out during a counselling session as to why I have absolutely zero control, but for now fuck it, let's focus on the comedy. Like the time I was trying to get out of my tuxedo when I was, shall we say *well-oiled*, after an awards ceremony and in an ill-fated attempt to take my trousers off whilst stood up I managed to lose my balance and book a one-way trip to the carpet. In my knee-jerk reaction of trying to put my hands down to stop myself face-planting the floor I got a finger caught in the belt loop and soon found not only was it a futile effort as my face got intimately acquainted with the carpet, but I'd also managed to dislocate said finger. What a shambles. I still remember looking at my wonky finger and being very confused as to why it was at such an odd angle, before trying to put it back in place. Thankfully being so drunk it wasn't that painful, but when I sobered up good lord it hurt like a motherfucker.

Anyway, back at the post-conference drinks I was surviving pretty well, and we'd just been told the plan was for the whole group to move to a local nightclub to continue drinking.

For some this was fantastic news - the chance to get in the club early and drink themselves silly without the fear of having to run the doorman gauntlet at a later hour when they'd definitely be refused entry for being absolutely shitfaced. For others it was surreal, for they'd either never been in a nightclub before 10pm or not been in one for donkeys' years. And for the rest, it was like they'd just been told they were being rounded up and loaded onto trucks destined for a Prisoner of War camp on the outskirts of Hull. Their faces quickly became very solemn, with some shaking their heads and whispering "Oh no…" as they processed what was happening and started to implement their escape strategies. We lost everyone over the age of 47 within six minutes.

Inside, the laws of the urban jungle were restored - no more boring work chat (namely because it was so loud you were reliant on basic words, lip-reading and the risky art of miming), lots of energy, and lots of mixing of drinks. Mixing wasn't always deliberate, mind you. A colleague came back from the bar with a round of drinks and after I protested at what he handed me he simply replied with "You asked me to get you a pint of Carling? Oh, sorry, I didn't hear you properly - here's a triple vodka and Coke instead."

By 10pm I was truly peacocking and having a glorious evening when suddenly Annabelle, the wolf in sheep's clothing from my time on the panel earlier, appeared and came over to have a drink and a chat with our group. She was all smiles and chatting away and then came over and stood next to me.

"How did you feel the session went earlier?" she asked.

Thinking she was about to lavish me with praise for the way I delivered the presentation and handled my time on the panel, I smiled and simply replied "I thought it went pretty damn well to be honest!"

I rapidly discovered she was not planning on lavishing me with praise. Nor was she planning on beating about the bush with some idle chit chat.

"Well I thought you came across as a bit of an arrogant cunt."

Wow. I was not expecting that.

"Erm, well, er… sorry, what?"

Realising that at the end of the day, she was still an industry leader and I had to maintain my company's reputation as well as my own, I tried to reason with her.

"I'm sorry if I caused any offence by the way I answered your question, I thought you were trying to shoot me down and I panicked," I quickly interjected.

But she was relentless.

"You were just sat there the whole time with that smug look on your face, like you're fucking better than everybody else," she spat at me. Pure venom. I felt like one of those snake charmers in rural India, shitting themselves as they tried to delicately move the violent and deadly creature as far away from them as possible without causing it to attack again.

"I am sorry," I continued, "I just wanted to be confident and happy, and if that's how it came across, I apologise."

It still didn't pacify the beast, and so the deadly dance continued for a further 20 bloody minutes - her cobra to my snake charmer engaging in a back and forth debate as to whether I really was a cunt or whether I was just a young guy trying to get by with a little bit of fake confidence. Quite a surreal situation to be in at 10:30pm in a half-empty nightclub. I'm normally getting called a cunt at 1am and promptly ejected just as it gets full. On that note I genuinely think they use me as a filler in bars and nightclubs, letting me in to help make it look busy and draw more people in, and then when people turn up who can actually dance, drink and not look like a hot sweaty mess I'm no longer needed. Being surplus to requirements I usually then get discretely ejected, usually by bouncers who are always dressed in tops two sizes too small for their hulking great bodies. I never understood that - why go so tight with your tops? Everyone can see you've got muscles on top of muscles. There's no need to look like a shrink-wrapped gammon joint.

Anyway, it got to the point with dear Annabelle where enough was enough - my friends had disappeared and I was just left standing there with her, missing out on the evening's fun. So, deciding honesty was the best policy and with me entering the jester phase, I decided to end the drama once and for all, and to do it with some panache. Leaning in closer to her, I softened my tone, and with a puppy dog look in my eyes I started my end game.

"It's okay, I get it," I started, "I completely understand. Look, I know we've not agreed, but I just want to say…"

She got hooked by my gaze and the sincerity in my voice, and leaned in closer. It was time to strike.

"… go fuck yourself."

And with that I wandered off with a spring in my step and the oh so sweet swagger reserved solely for people who have just done a mic-drop after coming out on top.

Let's be honest - I'd tried my best to defuse the situation, but sometimes you've just got to cut your losses and go "fuck it".

As I reached the edge of the room I turned to see how she'd taken it, and all I'll say is that my swagger was replaced with some wild-eyed speed walking to get to safety before the cobra could strike me down with her venom (aka the large glass of vodka and Coke she was about to launch).

The rest of the evening was its usual heady mix of too much shouting, awful dancing and drinking cocktails which tasted like they'd been made by a blind bartender specialising in homeopathy. I thought nothing more about my encounter with Annabelle - apart from wondering if I was suave enough to get away with any more retorts like that, before deciding that the kind of panache, smugness and downright dickheadedness it needed was only generated by a very specific set of circumstances (as well as an intake of alcohol which I was not keen to ever consume again) and that I was destined to be a run-of-the-mill guy when it came to exchanges like that one.

A few months later I ventured into London for a meeting with some of the leading technology companies in the UK to explore new ideas and ways to work together on new projects.

I looked across the room as the mass of grey suits assembled around the tables and there she was - sitting and smiling sweetly, like the fucking devil. Shit. "This isn't going to end well," I muttered under my breath.

During the introductions I learned that she was in actual

fact a very senior figure within a major organisation we needed to work with on a key project. Double shit.

Unsurprisingly, we didn't get the project.

This baffled everyone in my company, as they couldn't figure out why, but I sure as shit wasn't going to confess that I may have inadvertently been the cause.

Suffice to say, well done Annabelle - you did indeed manage to get one over me in the end... fucker.

Faux pas 26

The perils of X-ray vision

One of the highlights of the year when working for the engineering firm was an annual conference that we religiously attended.

This was an opportunity to head to far-flung places like Birmingham and other such jewels in the crown of this fine country and enjoy several days of talks, presentations, workshops and business dinners in order to learn about new technologies and practices which might further our nation's engineering capabilities.

Well, at least that's what we told our other halves and the colleagues who didn't get to go...

In reality, it was always several days of hanging out with team members we rarely got a chance to see, filling our pockets with merchandise snatched from other companies' stands, and at the end of each day heading out and getting gloriously wasted.

There are many a tale of hilarity, drunken stupidity and inappropriateness from these conferences, and as a veteran of nearly a dozen of these extravaganzas I've come to learn that every year there will, without fail, be some kind of incident which leads to someone skirting the fringes of constructive dismissal. Give us some examples, I hear you ask? Well, there's things like presenting whilst still drunk from the night before, missing the start of the conference from being so hungover, passing out drunk in front of senior management at dinner, and telling a manager to fuck off when asked to stay late to tidy up. There's then the embarrassing ones of forcefully trying to get into the wrong hotel late at night, being put to bed by a new colleague after passing out before 9pm, and suffering facial injuries by walking into a wall in a pitch-black hotel room whilst pissed.

Surprisingly though, this faux pas doesn't involve alcohol.

It was another classic conference - oversized halls illuminated by oversized lighting, which meant that the average engineer was suddenly presented with a hundred stands and their sales personnel manning them, and the horrendously stressful affair of having to pluck up the courage to walk over, introduce themselves and start a conversation. From the jittery movements and sweaty armpits it was clear this was a trigger for them, and they were experiencing some kind of PTSD from their teenage years when presented with the very same daunting and brightly-lit gauntlet known as the school disco.

It was absolutely brilliant watching these skittish little people scurry about, trying to avoid being accosted by a dreaded sales person before huddling in the safety of a group of other engineers who were bricking it at the thought of more social interaction. It was like watching a documentary on meerkats evading predators in the Kalahari Desert.

In fairness to the businesses that attended the conference they really did up their game over the years - the first one I went to was like a Parish Council meeting with little tables set up for pamphlets and free pens. In recent years it's taken on a real competitive element, with companies throwing some serious effort at their displays - ain't no Parish Council meetings going on with touchscreen displays, virtual reality headsets, Formula 1 cars or a free Pick n Mix stand. Yes, you heard right, free Pick n Mix. Well over 90% of the attendees unashamedly swarmed towards it like flies around shit when word of that got out.

At this particular conference I was manning one of our 'show and tell' stands, helping demonstrate some new kit we were trialling. Not being an engineer, I couldn't help but grimace a little when having to wax lyrical about the new kit we normally tested - grey box A with some wires being marginally smaller than grey box B and its bundles of wires, for instance, doesn't exactly set my world on fire, but for an engineer that is the stuff of steamy erotica. It really gets them going! They really should call engineering equipment catalogues Fifty Shades of Grey (Boxes). I remember once suggesting changing the styling of a device rather than anything technical and anyone would think I'd just suggested using tea towels to wipe our arses, such was the mocking I received. With more than a hint of David Brent from The Office, the comments of "Uh oh, someone wants to be in marketing," and "Why don't we just paint some go faster stripes on it?" left me crystal clear that you don't mess with the formula of grey boxes and grey wires.

This one particular year, though, we actually got to showcase something that did get me giddy with excitement. You see, this was the year when we were showcasing thermal imaging cameras. These devices were ridiculously sensitive - to the point where you could still see the residual heat left from someone's hand on a table a full minute after they'd moved it away, or even track their footprints on the carpet after they'd walked on it.

And so, much like the incident with the magnets many years before, my mind started to think of all the possibilities for mischief - and let's be honest, not a single one was ever going to be anything other than childish or inappropriate.

The thermal cameras themselves were like a pistol - it had a long handle, a trigger, a camera lense at the front and a display screen at the back to show you what you were aiming at. It was incredible to be able to point this thing at someone and see them represented on screen in a dazzling array of colours - blue for cold areas, red for warm, and white for hot hot hot. It was like being in a real-life version of Predator.

It was when aiming it like a gun at my friend Andy who was manning the stand with me that we realised this thing could effectively see through clothing… We guffawed like teenagers who were witnessing a topless sunbather for the first time. Although worryingly this was whilst pointing it at each others' crotch. But then I defy any man under the age of 30 to be given any kind of weapon and not at some point shoot it at another guy's balls. It was already pretty nerve-wracking manning the stands, with being on public display for days on end taking me back to the days of being a nervous teenager - wondering if my choice of clothing was shambolic, if my hair was okay, and if I had a forehead glistening like a glacier in the afternoon sun. But now add to this the fact that the state of my dick and balls could be determined by a quick glance through a thermal imaging camera and hey presto, I quickly turned into a bag of self-conscious nerves.

Case in point - whilst talking to an attractive visitor to the stand, I saw Andy a few metres away discretely pointing the camera at me and grinning, mouthing the words "You like her!"

Wrapping up the conversation pretty quickly I stormed over to him.

"What the fuck?" I berated him.

"Mate, I could see your crotch getting hotter the whole time you were talking to her," he laughed.

"What?! Bollocks," I shot back.

"Yeah that's what was giving off most of the heat," he giggled.

Smart arse.

This was it, I needed to get even and give him a reason to be nervous. And so the day went on, trying to catch each other out with some cheeky groin shooting - aiming the gun at one another and pulling the trigger as if firing a gun, pretending to shoot each other in the balls. I would feel ashamed at being so childish, but as I said before if I'm being honest I think every guy finds great delight in trying to strike another guy in the nuts. You can't shake it, from the day you can run to the day you die - boys will be boys.

But then it all started to unravel and our conference was threatened with coming to an early end - you see, what we didn't know was that pulling the trigger actually took a photo… and anyone could easily browse the photos which had been taken up to that point by simply clicking the left and right buttons below the screen on the back. So when delegates had finally mustered the courage to visit our stand and were busy checking out the kit, they were no doubt expecting to be able to see some demonstration shots showcasing the devices' capabilities on the classic grey boxes and wires. To everyone's horror, though, we all quickly realised that they were in fact being confronted with pictures of our red hot loins...

There are over 40 muscles in the human face. As a result, we can convey a wide array of emotions and responses to a given situation. From the look on the face of the person who first came across the nightmarish collection of phallic neon art, all 40 were working overtime to convey pure disgust.

In case you're wondering, yes, I took it personally. I mean, I understand it - a gentleman's appendage is not exactly a thing of beauty, but still… if being bathed in all the colours of the rainbow isn't enough to avoid someone's entire face grimacing in repulsion at the sight of it, then there's no hope.

Realising we needed to intervene immediately we strode over, feigning intrigue as to why they were looking so mortified. Thankfully we were able to paint a picture which placed the blame firmly on some unruly university students who were attending the conference, which was believable enough for them to tut and walk away, satisfied with our story. We quickly deleted the offending photos and breathed a sigh of relief, but we dreaded it was going to be our final hurrah in the company - I mean, it doesn't get much clearer cut for HR than an employee taking a picture of genitals on a company camera, does it?!

Dishonourable mentions

It goes without saying that I'm not the only idiot out there with a knack for saying the wrong thing at the wrong time, offending people, horribly misjudging situations and just generally fucking shit up.

I've had the pleasure of working with a fair few people who also fit that mould - we fuckwits come in all shapes and sizes, ages, genders, races and levels of affluence. Although it has to be said that some of my posher colleagues over the years have been so socially inept and unable to resist braying like a donkey at shit jokes with other Hooray Henries that they often featured in the awkward interaction history of my encounters. Bless them, they really struggled to hold their own in quick-fire banter with regular folks - I think it's thanks to their quips about Breitling watches and polo matches failing to land the same compared to when dished out amongst other wannabe Etonians.

But those awkward interactions were not particularly funny, they were just uncomfortable which isn't really worth shouting about. There are, however, a few other colleagues who have managed to tick both the funny and awkward boxes. So without going into full detail of my fellow fuckwits' faux pas (as they're very much their misadventures and not mine) I feel compelled to share the key details with you because they make me chuckle and I feel this is a nice little chapter to end on. It's kind of like having petit fours after a tasting menu because the gluttony of seven courses just wasn't enough - you still need something to definitively round off the meal (apart from the obscenely expensive bill).

My first honourable mention goes to a colleague who I was instant messaging, seeking a meeting to discuss something only for him to claim he was going to be busy for the next hour. I thought that was fair enough and agreed to set something up for an hour's time. But then an instant message from him popped up on my screen a mere five minutes later simply saying "sexy hot hooker cams". The little fucker had clearly brushed off my meeting request to have a cheeky *tommy tank*! He didn't type anything else after that, but he would have seen that I'd read the message. I didn't reply as I wanted him to squirm, with the tension lasting until the hour mark when I messaged him back and asked if he was free. Oh, and also if he'd found any good cams! He was suitably mortified. He was also rubbish with technology and failed to realise he could have simply deleted the message, making him both useless and a deviant. Not a good mix.

Next up is an exchange between two of the nicest ladies I've had the pleasure of working with, Siobhan and Vanessa. At a conference Vanessa had moaned about another team not listening to what she was asking them to do, to which Siobhan (in a misguided attempt at banter) had quizzed her "Is that because you're being a whiney little bitch?" Now if this had been thrown out to the guys or any of the other ladies who used to partake in such banter, then there would've been laughter all round. But Vanessa was not having a good day and so immediately called her out and tore into her in front of everyone like a mother scolding her child in public. We all felt uneasy witnessing it, especially as it continued for some time, leaving a rift between the two that lasted years. Unbeknown to them a few of us would use the phrase "Is it because you're being a whiney little bitch?" in workplace banter for a long time after that as it was a great quip to throw out unexpectedly!

Another mention goes to my dear colleague Fraser, a lovely guy from Aberdeen whose accent was so thick I often joked he needed subtitles for me to understand him. He gave great banter and was always good fun to be around. I actually worked for him for a little while and used to privately joke with him that I was a "spelling Nazi" as I was particularly good at proofreading reports and press releases. During one of his team meetings, the lovely Siobhan decided to correct him on his slack use of semicolons and so in an attempt to fire back some quick-witted banter he called her a "grammar Nazi". Normally, no problem at all. But Siobhan was half German, fiercely proud of it, and had a classic German surname to boot. "Er, really, Fraser? You really want to call me that?" she retorted. No, no he did not, and he was sheepish for the rest of the meeting, fearing he'd committed a hate crime and would soon be paid a visit by the HR grim reaper.

Or there was the time when I was doing the job fitting windows and doors and Danny called in sick one day, claiming he'd put his back out and couldn't move, only to bump into the co-owner in a shop the next town over, as they'd both inexplicably had to run an errand in the same place at the same time that day. There was no trust there at all after that, and you can imagine how things panned out when the work van started to have less fuel in it than the mileage warranted - Danny's word wasn't worth shit, and the questioning from the owners led him to quit in quite spectacular fashion.

An incident involving one of our company's business development teams took place whilst they were on a call with a German outfit who were trying to do a deal with ours - at one point during the call rather than go on mute the Germans simply spoke amongst themselves in their mother tongue. Unbeknown to them, one of our company's team spoke perfect German and learned that they thought we were stupid dickheads and they were planning to screw us over! The Director involved in the deal later took great joy in explaining why we were backing out of the deal, leaving them without any chance of getting their bonus that year.

Incredibly, at a Christmas party at the sales company one colleague got completely wasted and confessed to a senior manager in an ill-advised attempt to exchange cheeky secrets that he would occasionally use his toilet break to smash one out. Well I can tell you now that the only thing he was smashing after that were records for the number of job applications made in a single day after he was told to work elsewhere.

It should come as no surprise that at that same sales company another Christmas party had barely started before it became clear it was a clusterfuck of an event - an old boy called Rupert had been tasked with organising it, and after weeks of planning and much fanfare he had excitedly led the team into a conference room at a business centre on a Thursday afternoon in December. It turned out he had a very niche view of what a party should involve when it's for work colleagues. It was like being taken back in time to what must have been every office party in the

1970s - walking into the room there was simply a table in one corner with a stereo and speakers on it blaring out Christmas tunes, a table in another stacked high with nibbles and alcohol, and then two strippers in the middle of the room writhing around to Wham's Last Christmas. That was all the party consisted of! It was the last time poor Rupert was ever asked to organise any kind of social event for the company until he eventually retired a few years later.

My good friend Andy once decided after getting blind drunk that calling his boss up 'for a chat' at 3am would be a good idea. Undeterred by his boss hanging up, he proceeded to leave him a long, rambling drunken voicemail for when he woke up, full of chat about the quality of the ladies on the night out and how many shots he can knock back. He'd been with the company less than a year. He was politely asked to delete his boss' phone number from his personal phone as the best way to avoid pissing him off in future, and surprisingly managed to eek out another few years before he fucked it up and had to leave.

During an interview for a middle management position within our team one applicant was trying to paint us a picture of the energy crisis, but in his excitement his mouth was clearly a few steps ahead of his brain and instead of saying "dash for gas" we were treated to him blurting out "dash for gash"! His eyes went wide for a nanosecond before he powered on through and glossed over it. We didn't, however, and joked about it for some time afterwards.

Youngsters never cease to amaze me with taking instructions too literally, and not thinking them through.

Whilst hopefully none of them are still falling for being asked to go and get a tin of tartan paint, one of our subcontractors had a youngster complain of feeling a bit under the weather, and so was handed a tube of Berocca vitamin tablets and told to take one of those. He set off to drive down the motorway to another site, and when he arrived he had tears in his eyes and his shirt was covered in yellow stains. "What the hell happened?" the manager asked. Well, it turns out the poor lad had never heard of Berocca, and had no idea it needed to be placed in water and left to fizz away before drinking. He simply thought it was a chewable vitamin, and so whilst flying down the M4 he started to chomp on the effervescent tablet, only to start foaming at the mouth and promptly choking and crying as it did its thing. The silly sod was lucky he didn't crash!

Finally, it is fitting to end not so much with a faux pas but with a feat of sheer brilliance and balls (literally). Meeting up with a group of ex-colleagues down the pub one evening we were chatting about all the times over the years where people had courted controversy, and more often than not gotten away with it. After recounting some of the tales covered in these pages, colleague M (yes, that same cheeky little scamp I mentioned in the opening pages) decided to share with us that in the new world of working from home that followed the pandemic he and his girlfriend had been bored and frisky, and decided that him being on a conference call shouldn't stop them from getting it on. Cue M once again going at it like a rat up a drainpipe, albeit this time with someone much more his age, and more importantly with his headset still on! He apparently managed to finish both the deed and the call without any problems, causing several of us in the pub to actually applaud him and pat him on the back, like some kind of hero fighter pilot who returns to base after a successful mission. What a lad!

Self-reflection

Like being at some kind of yoga retreat, sharing my experiences has been extremely cathartic and not to sound too dramatic, but it's allowed me to reflect on my attitude to some of the major pillars in my life like work, friends and ultimately life itself.

It has been a funny, cringeworthy and at times surreal journey throughout my endeavours so far to carve out a career, and I hope you've enjoyed sharing in my faux pas - hopefully many of you can relate, and I've no doubt that many of you have much more awkward experiences under your belt.

It has to be said I've enjoyed working with everyone I've been colleagues with over the years (apart from one fiery South American...), and I appreciate those who didn't haul me over the coals for my indiscretions and instead let me continue to be free to cause mischief at every turn. For that, they are to be commended.

In reality, I've never been fortunate enough to have a career which truly hit the heights I dreamed of, but this is probably down to a combination of my own laziness and inability to avoid saying or doing the wrong thing. But then I think back to some of the most sage advice I've ever received, and whilst the fact it was written on a fridge magnet might take the shine off it for some, for me it matters not a jot, for never a truer word has been said - and it has continued to serve me well decades after I got it. The advice?

If you follow the rules all of the time, you'll miss all of the fun.

Not to sound like a career criminal, but often the most fun I've had has come from bending the rules, embracing the taboo, and at times simply not giving a shit. For those of you who strictly follow the rules/norms/expectations of society and the workplace, I encourage you to step out a little, cross that line every now and then and see how it can make things more fun, more exciting, and above all, funnier. What's the worst that can happen? If it goes well you'll have a great experience, and if it doesn't at least you'll end up with a great story to tell down the pub! Or the job centre if things really go south...

And for those of you who thought this was all too tame - just rein it in, you're probably one of the bellends that make people wish they'd applied for a different job or had different friends.

Much love,

Tom

Printed in Great Britain
by Amazon